KV-370-712

# Contents

# Employability

## SUSAN BLOCH
## TERENCE BATES

Published in association with  AMED

KOGAN
PAGE

## YOURS TO HAVE AND TO HOLD

### BUT NOT TO COPY

First published in 1995

Kogan Page Limited
120 Pentonville Road
London N1 9JN

© Susan Bloch and Terence Bates, 1995

**British Library Cataloguing in Publication Data**

A CIP record for this book is available from the British Library.

ISBN 0 7494 1786 2

Typeset by ghk Publishing Services, Chiswick, London.
Printed in England by Clays Ltd, St Ives plc

# Foreword by Sir John Egan

Every business succeeds by satisfying the needs of its customers. Managers have therefore to refresh continually their understanding of their customers' requirements and anticipate shifts in demand and expectations.

One thing does, however, tend to remain constant. Customers want good quality and low cost. So the managerial challenge is to deliver products and services efficiently, profitably and to high standards of quality so that the enterprise can prosper.

Of course all competitive businesses must also seek continually to raise their standards of customer satisfaction. The marketplace continues to widen, and in many sectors is already global, and the cost of entry to markets tends to decrease. Businesses must respond by continuously improving themselves.

These simple, even obvious, principles can be very difficult to put into practice, but in Britain we have now started to learn from the experience of others, such as Germany and Japan, by improving our managerial processes.

The most vital contributor to Continuous Improvement is the manager. All managers have to ensure that their own education and training is sufficient for the business challenges of both today and tomorrow. Relying solely on learning by experience on the job will leave too much to chance. The successful manager of the future will accept responsibility for his or her own development, and the development of their staff.

The Fast Track MBA series should be an invaluable aid to the manager who wants to improve personal performance and to plan for long-term success.

Sir John Egan
Chief Executive, BAA plc

# Introduction

## The world of the intellectual nomad

Careers need to be managed in much the same way as successful businesses. With a clear vision and strategy, your career will flourish and grow just as surely as a well-run business will succeed. It has always been true that education, skills and expertise need to be combined with a well-thought out career plan, but amid the changes now sweeping through the world of work, career management has become more crucial than ever before.

Employment patterns have changed out of all recognition in recent years, and the pace of change shows no signs of slowing down. As management structures are transformed, managers and professionals who might once have spent their entire careers climbing a single corporate ladder are suddenly discovering that the ladder itself has disappeared.

In this turbulent environment individuals are finding that they have to take responsibility for their own professional growth and learn how to build careers out of portfolios of skills and experiences. So if in the past you have looked to others for employment and direction, you will now have to find direction in yourself and employment in your own enterprise. You will need to think of yourself as an intellectual nomad, rooted in knowledge rather than in any one organization — and of the world as your marketplace.

This book will help you gain the skills necessary for navigating that journey into the unknown called a 'career'. The activities we have included will help you become mentally and physically fit for this journey and show you how to prepare for the unexpected. You will also learn how to become your own coach by developing a keen sense of self-awareness and actively managing your own personal development. As part of the MBA series this book will enable you to harness your intellectual knowledge and package it in a way that will put you on the road to success.

Throughout the book we encourage you to view your career as if it were a business: Me PLC. The activities we have included are designed to help you assess your strengths and weaknesses, establish strategic goals, develop your assets and market your 'unique selling points' (USPs). We believe that by applying these management techniques to your career, you will be able to achieve lifelong employ*ability* — even though lifelong employ*ment* in a single organization may no longer be a realistic goal.

# 1

# Choosing your own Future

## Living with change

Once upon a time choosing a career was a simple affair. In fact, with most people's 'careers' determined by their place of birth and their family's position in a stable social hierarchy, there was very little real choice. Skills were handed down from one generation to the next, and the son of the village blacksmith or thatcher would become a blacksmith or thatcher in his turn.

These people did not have 'jobs' in the sense that we have come to understand the word. They would shoe a horse or mend a roof when the need arose and receive payment for their services. But the notion of working for wages all the year round and using those wages to buy the necessities of life would have been entirely alien to most people in pre-industrial times. Though some were employed as servants to the wealthy, the majority lived and worked in households which produced most of their own food, clothing and domestic goods. The skilled artisan, when not plying his (or occasionally her) trade, would join in this activity. Even the landless peasant who sold his labour to others for a day or a season would not depend entirely on his wages, but grow some crops and raise a few sheep on the common land surrounding his village.

The social and economic upheavals known as the industrial revolution transformed these age-old working patterns — first in Britain and later in the rest of what we now call 'the West'. As the common lands were gradually enclosed by their owners and given over to intensive agriculture, much of the rural population began to migrate to towns and cities where newly-built factories were offering work in return for wages — in other words 'jobs' in the modern sense of the word. These changes affected not only the former landless peasants and artisans but also the members of a growing middle class who worked as clerks in the factories or in the professions servicing these new industrial enterprises.

By the end of the 19th century, waged employment had become the norm. Individuals were able to make choices about their careers, though for the majority of the population these choices remained limited, with society still assuming that the son of a doctor or a coal miner would follow in his father's footsteps.

A choice once made was usually for life, and for much of the 20th century people in the world's industrialized countries have expected to build their careers around one major skill and to spend their working lives within one organization. Organizations themselves operated on the same assumption. But as the century has progressed, physical and social mobility have increased and so has the rate of change in occupational roles. Expectations of a job for life in one organization have almost gone, and even the concept of a single life-long career is now loosening its hold. According to some commentators, we are now witnessing a revival of older working patterns, with people no longer necessarily *having* jobs but *doing* them as and when demand for their labour, skills or knowledge arises.

The future, in other words, is already here and it is one of change at least as great as that which so bewildered our forebears in the late 18th and early 19th centuries. Our aim in this book is to help you equip yourself to lead the life you want in this future.

You may feel that with so much uncertainty, you have even less control over your future than the medieval peasant had over his or hers. Yet even in pre-industrial times there were some individuals who left home, crossed kingdoms, acquired learning and achieved positions in society far removed from their origins. They were driven by a desire for something other than what fate seemed to have ordained for them. The same motivation is essential whether in a society that is fixed and stable or one that is as fluid and uncertain as our own — essential, that is, unless you are content to accept whatever fate deals for you.

## Me PLC

Why is it that so many people settle for what they have or what they are doing, while wishing that things could be different? The answer is time: most people do not devote nearly enough of it to consciously managing their careers. Working hard at a job, seeking further qualifications, striving for promotion and showing commitment to an organization are all aspects of career management. It is easy to assume that by doing these things you are managing your career — and in any case you may feel that there is not much more you can or need to do about it. If you need another job, then it may be enough simply to focus on advertisements, applications and interviews. But there is much more to career management than that.

Managing your career can usefully be viewed as running a business. Think of yourself as Me PLC and you can apply concepts such as vision, mission, objectives, assets, and stakeholders to your career. That way you can see yourself as employing your current or future employers to meet your own needs, a new perspective that will enable you to assess the extent to which you are on track and how far you may need to change in order to develop and enhance your employability.

As we know, all businesses need more than good day-to-day management. Without a strategy, corresponding research, and the development of its assets — all of which can be ignored in the short term — a business will eventually flounder.

The same goes for a career. Take as an example an individual we will call Marion. She started her career as an accounts clerk in a City bank and worked hard year after year until, at the age of 40, she had risen to a senior position in financial control. However, she has just been moved to a new role and is no longer happy as it is less central to the core of the business than her old job. She would like to leave the bank, but every job advertisement she sees asks for accountancy qualifications.

Marion never did qualify, which did not hold back her progress in an organization where she was well known and respected. But she now finds that this is a major obstacle to finding a new position. Marion, in other words, has failed to invest in the development of a major asset: a professional qualification.

## Not another one

By now you may be asking what is so special about this book and how it can help you. 'I have invested in my career, I've taken the long view and whatever happens, I will be OK. I don't need to do anything other than do a good job and as far as I can see there are enough self-help books around already. How is this one different?'

We believe this book is different because while the theory of managing a career is essentially simple common sense, the practice can be more difficult. We have therefore largely avoided the use of questionnaires and inventories and adopted instead an approach that encourages you to clarify the direction you wish to take by searching among the variety and uniqueness of your own preferences and aspirations. We recognize that this process will take time and that each individual will wish to come up with his or her own chosen route.

To find your route to employability and career success you will need to assess both your short and long-term objectives. You will also choose the extent to which you use the book and you will choose — as you already have done — what you will continue to do with your life. Our basic position is this: IF IT IS TO BE, IT IS UP TO ME.

Whatever has happened to you, is happening to you or will happen in the future comes down to your own choice. It may not always have *felt* like that, but wherever you are now in life, we suggest that the sensible course is to decide that from now on you will consciously and actively manage your own career and your own life.

## Using this book

Apart from the book, all you need is a large file with dividers to keep the output from the activities you will be doing. You will also need to keep a notebook with you at all times to jot down your thoughts or observations: active career management means that your mind will be in a state of alert and you will need to record such thoughts and observations as they occur.

We urge you to tackle the activities as you come to them. Each involves some writing and may take up to an hour, though we recommend that you revisit them as your thinking about the future develops. This book will be of almost *no* benefit to you unless you carry out the activities!

You will derive additional benefit from working with a partner, sharing and discussing thoughts and reactions. If you decide to do this, ask each other questions but do not argue or criticize. Aim to provide each other with mutual support and encouragement; meet on a regular basis to share progress and to provide each other with an incentive to complete each exercise before the next meeting.

Finally, bear in mind that this book will not help you find quick and easy answers — because there are none. Managing your career is a process that continues throughout life. Your focus and direction can change, your objectives may alter and you will abandon some aims.

Successfully managing your career is more about travelling than about arriving. For this reason the activities we have included to help you on this journey are in the main open-ended. They are designed to help you reflect and increase your awareness of who you are and what it is you *really* want to do. Only you can answer these questions and only you can assess the validity of what you have written down.

But before you get started, we will look ahead to the 21st century to attempt to envisage what the world of work and employment will be like. All the indications are that if career management has been important up to now, it will be *essential* in the future.

## Careers in the 21st century

We have already mentioned the continuously changing and flexible future which faces us all in the next century. Organizations are no longer the relatively secure and stable places they were over the last few decades. The concept of a job for life in the same company, whether it be a large monolith like Shell or IBM or a small local factory or shop, is fast becoming obsolete. The idea that an organization will plan your career and take care of you is also seriously flawed — though, as the following case study shows, it may still lurk in our heads.

### Case study: Shifting responsibilities

Graham worked for a large company established well before the Second World War and now a world leader in its field. For many years the company had been run on paternalistic, quasi-military lines, many of its employees having been in the armed services. There was a tradition of long service often covering two or three generations of the same families. 'Career management' was largely a question of job placement governed by fixed ideas about the number of years an individual should be in a job before a move or promotion occurred.

Graham, who was seen as a loyal and competent manager, reached a senior level as head of a small unit providing specialist services to the rest of the organization. He wanted to remain in this job but after six years the company's senior management decided that change was needed. Graham was aggrieved by this decision and even more disturbed to discover that he was expected to find his next job by promoting himself and networking throughout the organization.

Eventually he found a position in quite a different field, managing the company's community relationships. This was a high profile job requiring a very different range of skills and behaviours from those that had enabled him to succeed in his previous role.

The issue for the company was that while it did not want to lose Graham, he had to demonstrate that he had the flexibility to seek out new opportunities for himself. Times had changed and career moves were no longer instigated by the personnel department. The balance had shifted, turning career management into the responsibility of the individual as much as the organization.

Careers in the future may be best described as mosaics or jig-saws which individuals piece together as they acquire a wide variety of experiences not necessarily related to each other in the linear fashion of old. In other words, people's working lives will consist of portfolios of skills, qualifications and roles rather than a series of discrete and easily defined jobs.

Various writers (particularly Charles Handy, Peter Drucker and William Bridges) have attempted to predict the career patterns of the future. Their views and those of others encompass a bewildering range of sometimes apparently contradictory possibilities, with, on the one hand, predictions of growing economic globalization and, on the other, of the rapid spread of 'teleworking' from 'electronic cottages'. Nevertheless, there are trends that consistently emerge and, in many cases, these are already with us.

We shall do no more than list these trends here and draw some conclusions for personal career management strategy.

The first major theme is of discontinuous change: predictions about individual careers are no longer possible as organizations themselves find it difficult to know what will happen in two or three years' time.

Secondly, the structure of organizations is becoming much more fluid as continuous re-engineering results in temporary project teams handling an increasing number of tasks and corporate ladders give way to career lattices. The seemingly never-ending improvements in information technology make possible achievements that were in the realms of science fiction only a few years ago. Power and information no longer lie in the hands of a few individuals at the top of an organization. The traditional hierarchy has ceased to be — if it ever were — a valid representation of the relationships and processes undertaken in any organization.

Turning to individual skills and abilities, the picture is much the same — at whatever level, whether that of the manual worker or the research scientist, the rate of change in materials, techniques and information available is relentless. The world is less forgiving too: in the old-style organization you could hide or make do with a job for which you were only partly suited — but that is no longer the case.

The pressures to perform well and to focus on the measurement of individual behaviour are strong as every organization becomes increasingly focused on quality, leaving far less room for slack in the system.

The impact of these developments for each individual is clear. You can no longer take chances with your career or assume that by simply doing a good job, you will ensure your future success. As Peter Drucker has said, you can no longer design your life around a temporary organization.

As an individual developing your career in the 21st century, you will need to understand and learn to manage these issues, which we have summarized below as a series of paradoxes.

1.   The need to maintain and develop a core of skills and abilities, while also being able to manage and work in a series of very different contexts and cultures.

2.   The need to be self-centred and independent while being able to work with teams and groups in a collaborative way.

3.   The ability to cope with high pressure and short time scales while keeping a range of interests and a life-style that is both healthy and satisfying.

4.   The ability to spend periods as a manager and as a 'doer', to move laterally or even 'downwards', to be self-employed for some of the time and employed at other times.

5.   An outlook which will enable you to be committed, enthusiastic and 'loyal' and yet to deal with the inevitable when you are no longer required by a particular organization.

6.   The ability to think globally but act locally.

We conclude this chapter with a case study that looks at the shape of careers to come.

## Case study: A portfolio career

When Gareth left university with a good honours degree in economics he had high hopes of a life-long career in banking. At first all went according to plan, and he secured a coveted place on a graduate training scheme at one of the City of London's oldest and most prestigious investment banks.

He made rapid progress and soon joined the bank's management cadre. Meanwhile, his personal life was also going well, and five years after joining the bank he married Sandra, a fellow employee. Their working days were long, but at weekends they were able to indulge their passion for sailing. At the end of one of the bank's most successful trading years, their combined bonuses enabled them to buy a small yacht.

It was while Sandra was on maternity leave after the birth of their first child that catastrophe struck. A financial fraud on a spectacular and unprecedented scale led to the collapse of the bank, taking with it not only their jobs but also their savings. Gareth and Sandra were forced to sell the yacht, as well as their home in one of London's smartest districts.

Gareth spent several months looking for a job in another bank, but with the whole banking sector in turmoil following his previous employer's collapse, this search proved fruitless. Eventually he began to take stock of his skills and abilities and to think about what kind of work he might be able to do outside the banking arena. Within weeks he had found a job as an instructor in a sailing school. He, Sandra and the baby moved to the small town on the south coast of England where the school was based.

Although Gareth was now earning just a fraction of his former salary, it was, as he said to sceptical friends, a living — and a thoroughly enjoyable one at that. It also led to other things. One of the people Gareth instructed in sailing was a senior manager in a leading building society. The society was in the process of merging with another player in the financial services market, and Gareth heard through his contact that the organization was putting together a temporary project team to manage aspects of the merger. He approached the building society and was awarded a six-month contract, later extended to a year.

The contacts he established during this period have enabled Gareth to build up a new career in project management. Whereas he once envisaged a career in which he would climb steadily up a corporate ladder, he is now using and developing an ever-widening portfolio of skills. When more lucrative work is scarce, his old boss at the sailing school is happy to take him back for the odd day or week. In the winter months when the school is closed Gareth sometimes works alongside Sandra, who has established her own second career as an independent financial adviser.

There is a growing population of professionals who are becoming better and better at managing portfolio type careers. These may be in the same line of work as that in which the individual was previously employed, as in Sandra's case in the above case study. Other portfolio careers may consist of periods of employment and self-employment in more than one occupational area, as in Gareth's case.

# 2

# Where have you got to?

## A personal 'SWOT' analysis

Deciding what you want from your life requires the development of a vision or series of visions. These will consist of images of what you are doing, where, with whom and in what circumstances. Some of you reading this may already have formed such images. Others — and, we suspect, the majority — will be less clear. In this and the next chapter we will show you how to focus on the future and develop a vision by first charting the past and defining the present.

The activities in this chapter will enable you to carry out an audit of where you are now — a kind of personal SWOT analysis (strengths, weaknesses, opportunities and threats). You should find that the act of writing down where you are now in the main areas of your life — career, relationships, interests and personal development — will start you thinking about how to describe the future that you want. The required frame of mind for these activities is that of an objective observer who knows all there is to know about you!

### Activity 1: Where are you now in your career?

Write the above question on the first page of your notebook. In this, the first activity, your objective is to describe in some detail what you are doing now in your career. Write your account in simple and clear terms that would be understood by someone who knew nothing about your job or how you currently earn your living. If you are not in paid employment at the moment, write about your last job.

You may find it helpful to use the following headings as a framework:

- the key tasks of your job

- its objectives and overall purpose

■ the scope of your responsibilities

■ who you work for and who your 'customers' are

■ your level and status in the organization

■ the opportunities for advancement

■ the relationships that you have at work.

Keep your description factual and as objective as possible. Do not indicate how much you like or dislike what you do or how successful you are; later activities will give you opportunities to evaluate your own performance and your feelings about what you are currently doing.

This activity has two purposes. First, the expression of where you are now is essential for planning the future. Secondly, the ability to describe simply and accurately what you do is an essential career management skill, which will be of particular value when you are in meetings or interviews where the aim is to promote and present yourself or your 'products'.

## Activity 2: Taking stock of finances and assets

Like all enterprises, 'Me PLC' needs to ensure that its finances are under control. In this activity, therefore, we ask you to produce a factual account both of your outgoings and of the material assets available to you.

You may find it helpful to use the following headings as a guide.

### Income and expenditure (cash flow)

■ your income from employment and any other sources

■ your expenditure broken down into:
    a) essential expenditure (food, heating, payments on loans and the like);
    b) desirable and leisure expenditure (interests, holidays, eating out, extra clothing and so on); and
    c) the amount you save each month or the extent to which you are in deficit at the end of each month.

## Wealth

■ assets in terms of:
   a)   savings
   b)   possessions
   c)   the value of any property you own (not forgetting how much you owe)
   d)   anticipated inheritance.

When you have completed this personal 'profit and loss' account, carry out a further check on your personal financial management by answering the following questions.

■ Are you managing on your income or are you spending more than you earn?

■ What plans do you have to meet your debts? Are they scheduled effectively, at minimum interest rates, with any pledged assets sufficient to cover loans?

■ Are you up to date with your tax returns? Have you reserved sufficient funds to meet future tax bills?

■ Are you covered for possible disasters such as health problems, long-term incapacity, fire, accident and theft?

■ Is your will up to date?

■ Are you prepared financially for retirement?

■ If your finances are separate from your partner's, are you both clear about each other's specific responsibilities?

■ If you have savings, are they held in tax-efficient vehicles?

■ Do you read the newspapers' financial pages to keep up to date with developments affecting your personal finances?

It is important that you complete this activity. Knowing where you are in material terms is clearly important as a framework for future decisions. In addition, the choices you have already made about wealth and possessions are a reflection of your personality and motivation.

## Activity 3: What happens when you are not working?

We now ask you to describe how you spend your time when you are not engaged in paid work. Write about what you do in the evenings, on days off, weekends and so on, and how often you like to carry out particular activities. Include the time you spend with your family or the people with whom you live and with friends.

Your description should cover:

■ family

■ other relationships

■ interests and hobbies (including sports and keeping fit)

■ reading (books, magazines and newspapers)

■ watching television and listening to the radio

■ holidays

■ studying and attending classes

■ voluntary and community work

■ cultural activities (films, theatre, opera and the like)

■ religious or other spiritual activities.

Try to estimate how much time you devote to each of these activities. You may feel that you are not spending as much time as you would like on some of them. Once again, your choices in these areas indicate aspects of motivation that you may not be aware of — or provide insights into the need to manage your time more effectively. If you are at a crossroads in your career, you may also find that your leisure interests and activities can help you strike out in a new direction — which is what happened to the former executive who is the subject of the following case study.

## Case study: Third age career

John came from a working-class background and was brought up in one of the most deprived areas of a large city. However, he did well at school and subsequently at technical college, where he studied electrical engineering on day release from a small company. On qualifying, he joined a major British company and made steady progress through a variety of jobs. After gaining both workshop and field service experience, he joined the firm's management team, eventually rising to a position where he was responsible for more than 100 members of staff.

At the age of 52, John's world was shattered when his company merged with one of its competitors and his opposite number was preferred for the job that he had hitherto held. John was extremely distressed about this decision and made no attempt to disguise his feelings. He had little desire to look for similar employment elsewhere — which, in any case, would have been extremely difficult for him to find in the poor economic climate of the time.

Ever since his childhood, John had enjoyed working with his hands and was known to his family and friends as something of a wizard when it came to repairing cars, household appliances and virtually any other type of machine. Once his shock at losing his job began to abate, he was able to start thinking about what he wanted to do with the rest of his life. He decided to look for work that would make use of his well-developed practical skills. He also realized that he was not concerned with status, though he was keen to do 'something useful' for his local community.

Initially, John was able to meet these aspirations by taking on unpaid work as a handyman for a local charity. Then, as time went on and the need to start contributing to the family budget became pressing, he decided that someone with his skills could be of value in an educational institution, perhaps as a laboratory technician. He began to make enquiries and applied for several jobs.

One of the problems he encountered was that people would not take him seriously or else assumed that he wanted the boss's job! But he did eventually find a position as a university laboratory technician and rapidly proved that he could do the job — and more. The laboratory has never been run more efficiently, various long-abandoned pieces of equipment have been repaired and John feels that he is probably of greater material benefit to society than he has ever been in his life.

John's remarkably successful adaptation to a new working life style shows that individuals who cultivate self-awareness and an insight into their own motivation can strike out in a new direction at any stage of their lives.

## Activity 4: How satisfied are you?

As you tackled the first three activities in this chapter, it must have been difficult to keep in check your desire to express satisfaction or the lack of it. Now is your chance. Describe how contented or satisfied you are with each of the following aspects of your life:

■ your work and career

■ your relationships

■ your material wealth and possessions

■ your non-work activities and interests.

Be honest with yourself and try to describe your feelings as they really are. Write about how you feel *now* — not about what your aspirations might be. To start with, draw a scale of 0 to 10 from complete dissatisfaction to perfect contentment and evaluate each of the above aspects of your life on this scale.

When you find that satisfaction is high or low, try to define in specific terms what it is that leads to these feelings. For example, if you are dissatisfied with your job, decide if the dissatisfaction is with:

■ the work itself and the tasks involved

■ your relationships with others, including bosses, colleagues and people you manage

■ your relationships with customers, clients or suppliers

■ the culture or style of the organization

■ your conditions of employment, including pay and benefits.

## Case study: A change of direction

Robert, aged 35, carried out the above activity in some detail. A specialist in aspects of management information and control who wrote and lectured on his subject, he had rarely stayed in one company for longer than three years.

The notes he made to analyse his feelings about his current role helped him recognize that while he found the work itself deeply satisfying, he had difficulty in handling relationships with other senior managers. Clashes were a regular occurrence and it did not help that Robert thought he was usually right!

Although he had always valued job security, Robert now decided that he would become an independent consultant. His aim was to develop further as a leading authority in his specialism, to carry out research and publish articles. He also planned to establish links with business schools and large companies with a requirement for advanced mathematical modelling.

Robert's experience suggests that the process of examining the factors that give individuals satisfaction in their working lives can help them identify the kind of work they are likely to find most congenial.

## Case study: A change in emphasis

Caroline, a senior accountant encouraged to examine her feelings about her role, realised that the activities which gave her most satisfaction always had something to do with other people: developing her team, running meetings, dealing with clients and making presentations. This realization indicated that it might be a good idea for her to pursue a role in general management rather than the one she currently held in taxation. Having discussed her new aims with her company's human resources director and enlisted his support, she recently enrolled on a part-time MBA programme.

Caroline too had taken the time to discover what she most enjoyed doing, and as a result succeeded in steering her life in a new direction.

Remember that satisfaction and dissatisfaction are not 'global'. They are outcomes of particular features of the situations you are in and the way you handle those situations. Asking yourself searching questions about how you feel about the various aspects of your life and giving specific answers is the first step in deciding what action to take next — but more of that later.

## *Activity 5 - Wishes and aspirations*

The final activity in the 'where are you now?' audit is to take stock of your wishes and aspirations for the future. We will return to the future in other activities later in the book, but the aim is to capture quickly and spontaneously what is in your head now.

Do this exercise as a *brainstorm*. Anything goes — do not evaluate the likelihood or practicability of any of your wishes. If these wishes exist now, they are telling you something about your current state and should not be ignored or rejected.

## 1 Career aspirations

Write down as much as you can about where you believe you want to get to. Focus on the following:

- the type of work you would like to do

- the skills you would need to use or develop

- the level and status you would like to reach

- the scale and type of organization you would like to work in

- the type of employment you would like: self, portfolio, contract or 'permanent'.

Do not worry if any of this conflicts with what you are actually doing now, or if it indicates that you will need to change direction and learn new skills.

## 2 Relationships

Express your wishes and aspirations about the sorts of relationships you would like to have with:

- friends and partners

- family and children

- people at work

■ people in the community

■ people who share your hobbies and interests.

## 3  Non-career activities

Describe what you would like to achieve, experience, learn about and enjoy during the rest of your life. Use the following headings as a framework:

■ interests and hobbies

■ reading and learning

■ holidays and travel

■ community involvement

■ sports and fitness

■ voluntary work

■ political activity

■ spiritual or philosophical thinking.

When tackling the above activities, do not be cautious or restrictive but aim to include all your dreams and aspirations. You will find that compiling these lists over several days gives your mind the opportunity to get to work.

## A break in the journey

By now you should have filled quite a few pages with notes and more extended writing. You will find that in reviewing what you have done so far, new thoughts and ideas will occur to you and they will continue to occur as you return to these notes from time to time. Perhaps this is the first time in your life that you have allowed yourself the luxury of spending a few hours thinking about yourself in a relatively systematic way. Aim to devote a couple of hours every week to this activity.

As we have pointed out already, career and life planning is a process rather than an act; it is evolutionary and continuous. Too often, in our experience, people either do not plan their lives and careers at all or, if they do, it is in response to some external, unplanned event such as the appearance of an advertisement or a crisis such as redundancy.

As a result of what you have written, you are already better prepared to react to opportunities or to respond more effectively to adverse circumstances. You should be finding that you are more aware of yourself and what you are doing in your career. You are probably also paying more attention to information you come across about the changing world of work whether in newspapers, on radio or television or in conversation with friends and colleagues. This open, inquisitive frame of mind is an essential attribute for the effective career manager — but there is more work to be done. These first few activities are the groundwork that will enable you to move on to the next stage: an analysis of how you have got to where you are today and how you have developed your unique set of skills, abilities and attitudes.

# 3

# How did you get there?

## Understanding the past

In the last chapter we helped you take a snapshot of where you feel you are today. The next step is to look back and record what has brought you to the present stage in your life and career. If you are to construct the future that you want, an understanding of your past is essential. What you are now is a product of all that has happened to you. The influences will have been many, including family, schooling and the places where you have lived. Some of these influences will come from events that you have long forgotten; others will come from events that, while clearly remembered, may have affected you in ways you do not at the moment recognize.

There are no direct or simple relationships between past experiences and current behaviour. Each person is a unique product of the interactions between genetic inheritance, his or her actions and choices, and external circumstances. That said, it is possible for most people to look back and recall what seem to be the major influences on their attitudes, beliefs and behaviour.

You may still be wondering why you are being asked to look at your past in such detail — after all it is your future career that is your main concern. Apart from increasing your awareness of yourself, these exercises will:

- enable you to understand the extent to which you have already made choices about your career

- help you to locate the situations, environments and tasks in which you feel most comfortable and effective

- increase your understanding of your skills and attitudes in dealing with people

- call to mind events and achievements that may well be of great relevance in meetings and interviews still to come.

## Activity 1: The early days

The way to begin to understand the influences that have helped to shape your personality is, once again, to write about them! This time, we are asking you to write an autobiography. We shall provide a structure and a series of questions that will enable you to make rapid progress. You can answer these questions in note form if you wish.

Start with your earliest memories. Who and what do these concern?

Then lead into a description of the first few conscious years of your life up to the age of about seven or eight. Think about:

- where and with whom you were living

- what the house and locality were like

- what your parents or guardians were like, how you remember them, how you feel you were treated and what you remember about other people such as grandparents, uncles and aunts

- brothers and sisters, if any, or other children you were close to, their ages and positions in the family, and how you feel you got on with them

- your first day at school and how you felt about it, what you thought about the teachers

- the next few years at school, your favourite subjects, how you felt you were doing and how you were treated by others

- your friends, your 'play time', your interests.

## Activity 2: The teenager

The next section will cover the years up to your early teens and include:

- schooling and changes of school, why these occurred and how you felt about them

- the subjects you preferred and why you chose them

■    how you were judged by teachers, and how you felt about these judgements

■    your first examinations

■    other activities you took part in at school

■    out-of-school activities and interests

■    changes in the membership of your family

■    how you felt about parents and other adults in the family network

■    your earliest ambitions and ideas on careers

■    friends of both sexes.

## Case study: A late developer

Sylvia's story illustrates how an understanding of early experiences can help individuals clarify goals and aspirations in adult life.

The youngest child of immigrant parents from eastern Europe, Sylvia is 31 years old. Her parents, who have run the same small shop for over 30 years, were always ambitious for their two sons, one of whom is now a university lecturer while the other is a partner in a well-known firm of solicitors. Sylvia, on the other hand, was encouraged to think of herself as a future wife and mother. Growing up in a close and loving family with few social contacts other than relatives, she did not question these assumptions.

Sylvia cannot remember having any ambitions at school and left with just a few 'O' levels, having shown no particular aptitude for any academic subject other than English literature. Her parents did not teach their native tongue to any of the children but as an adult Sylvia developed an interest in languages, attended evening classes and can now 'get by' in several European languages.

After taking a secretarial course at a local college in her late teens, Sylvia held several clerical jobs. However, her increasing dissatisfaction with these jobs led her to seek vocational guidance. The results of the intelligence and aptitude tests she took as part of this process showed her to be in the top 10 per cent of the adult population in terms both of general intelligence and linguistic aptitude. She took time to absorb the implications of these results and at first thought there had been some mistake.

Later Sylvia began to recall her school days and to think about how her own limited aspirations and the expectations of her family had prevented her from fulfilling her potential. Meanwhile her current employer had clearly spotted her ability and put her in charge of a unit of 12 people who produced written reports based on consumer surveys. This new responsibility gave her greater satisfaction than she had previously found in her work, but she began to see that she would never feel fully satisfied unless she returned to her early interest in literature. Her intention now is to study for an Open University degree in English and she is already halfway through the foundation course. She is not concerned that the subject is non-vocational, and is content to stay for the time being in her current job. For Sylvia, academic achievement is important as a validation she did not experience in adolescence.

Like Sylvia in the above case study, you may find that the process of self-analysis gives you the understanding to grow into the person you want to be — and to make the right career choices.

## Activity 3: First career choices

Now look at the period from your mid-teens to the time you took up your first job. Include:

■ your school record, what subjects you studied and why, the examinations you took and how you felt you were doing

■ your choice of subjects for further study and the reasons for this choice

■ the people who were the main influences on you at this time and how they influenced you

■ other activities that took up your time at this stage, including jobs, holidays, interests.

■ your time in further or higher education, if appropriate; why you chose the subjects you studied, how you did in them and how you spent the rest of your time as a student

■ your first job; how and why you got it and what it entailed.

## Activity 4: Your career to date

Continue your life history by writing about what has happened to you since your first job. Including job titles, responsibilities, achievements and dates will turn this task into essential preparation for the production of your curriculum vitae. By describing significant incidents in your career to date, you will also ensure that you are not stuck for words when an interviewer asks you about your past achievements.

Take each job in turn and make a note of:

■ the title, responsibilities and purpose of the job

■ your achievements

■ what you learnt

■ how you felt about the job

■ what led to changes and/or promotion.

At the same time, write about what was happening in other areas of your life, including:

■ friendships and relationships

■ interests and leisure activities

■ study and learning.

When you have finished this activity and the activities included in the last chapter, you will have conducted a survey of your life so far. We hope you have enjoyed carrying out this survey! There will probably have been memories that were pleasant to recall and others that were more painful. An additional activity will help you identify how satisfied you are with your life to date.

## Activity 5: Lifeline

Draw a line representing your life across the middle of a page. Divide it into five year segments. Take key events and note them above or below the line, depending on whether you view them in a positive or negative light.

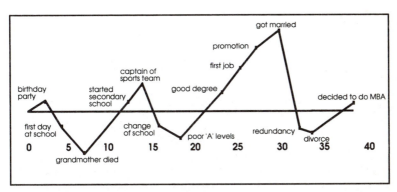

Summarise the high and low points and record what you have learnt from them. What would you do now if a similar event occurred — would your behaviour be different? Are there any patterns beginning to emerge?

## Activity 6: A look at past choices

The aim now is to learn from all that you have done so far in this chapter and the last one. Our intention is to help you develop an understanding of why you have done the things you have done and which ones have given you satisfaction. To do this you will need to review your notes and pick out key events. Consider the following:

■ choices that you made or were made for you

■ events that 'happened' to you

■ achievements that brought you satisfaction

■ transitions from school to school or job to job.

List these down one side of a page as shown below. Then summarise why you made key choices and whether you found certain achievements satisfying and others frustrating or annoying.

| Event | Influence/choice |
|---|---|
| *Going to secondary school* | Had no choice — forced on me — but felt OK about it. |
| *Change of secondary school* | Again, had no choice — family moved because of father's job. Disliked new school and felt very unhappy at leaving old friends. |
| *First job* | Attracted by company's good name and chance to travel. |
| *Redundancy* | Forced on me. Felt cross but relieved. Company in a bad way. I should have left two years earlier. |
| *Degree course* | Wanted to do something that was not a 'school subject' and had a vocational aspect. Felt I was doing something for myself at last! |

Now answer the following questions:

■ What can you learn from carrying out the above exercise about how to make the best choices for the future?

■ What kinds of choices should you avoid making?

■ To what extent have you been influenced by other people and external events or by extrinsic factors such as pay, conditions and status?

■ To what extent have your own feelings, preferences and intrinsic interests determined your choices?

■ What have you learnt about your flexibility and adaptability? How have you coped with choices or events that were unsatisfactory?

■ Can you identify and describe any general themes, patterns or ways in which you have changed?

## Case study: The wrong choices

An ambitious executive we shall call Jane felt uncomfortable after completing the above exercise. She began to realise that some of the choices she had made for what appeared to be good, logical career reasons had also led to the disruption of her personal relationships.

Jane was brought up in a caring family but one where her parents worked hard six or seven days a week running the grocer's shop they owned. Her own adult life has followed the same pattern of putting work first. She decided to study at a university three hundred miles from home because it offered the 'best' course in her chosen subject, even though her parents were worried about the distance. Later in her first job she worked all hours while also studying for a part-time MBA. Her current commitment of all her free time to a voluntary organization is another example of this behaviour.

She now realizes that her increasing discontent stems from the fact that she has very few close friendships. Though still deeply committed to her career, she has decided to take account of personal and social factors when making future career decisions. Her own family had always evaluated choices in simple, pragmatic terms, but she now recognizes that there is more to weighing up options than to ask herself, as she had done in the past: 'Will this help me get on?'

# 4

# Unpack your kitbag

## Do you know what's in there?

As we go through life we all acquire a host of skills, knowledge and experiences. While it is this 'kitbag' full of expertise that enables us to progress further, all too often we are not aware of what exactly it contains. In this chapter we will help you examine the contents of your own kitbag and so gain a better understanding of your strengths and weaknesses. This is an important process because there is a strong connection between your grasp of the factors that have influenced your career progression so far and your ability to manage a career change or transition to a new role. Only by recognising your own abilities and achievements, as well as all the potentially available opportunities, will you be able to define your own future — and gain the confidence to reach out for it.

Reviewing your career to date, however, will not take you any closer to fulfilling your ambitions unless you are also able to describe past achievements and successes to others in a positive and effective way. Simply explaining the ups and downs in your career in terms of luck or the opportunities that have come your way will not do. A later chapter in this book will look at self-marketing — the art of letting others know what you have achieved; but for now we will focus on the basis of that art and help you gain further insight into your own achievements.

### Activity 1: Vignettes: the key to the contents

To begin to develop this insight, you will need to review many of the steps you have taken during your working life. We suggest you do this by producing a series of 'vignettes' to describe your past achievements. Each vignette should include:

■ an outline of the situation you faced

■ a description of the action you took to influence the situation, and

■ a note of the result or yield of that action.

Begin by considering what you have achieved in your current or most recent role and then work your way backwards in time. Review the notes you have already made, think carefully and try to make sure you do not leave out any significant successes. You may like to ask colleagues, former colleagues, friends or family to help jolt your memory.

Model your vignettes on the following examples.

### Vignette 1

In reviewing one of his achievements, Peter, the managing director of a pharmaceutical company, made the following notes.

Situation: The company's dental product range had a very low profit margin.

Action: Peter took steps to have the end item range reduced by pruning and redesign. He also ordered a review of the firm's production process. This revealed that rigid demarcation lines were slowing down work by preventing machine operators from carrying out routine maintenance work on manufacturing equipment. By negotiating a new agreement with the two trade unions representing operators and skilled craftsmen, Peter was able to eliminate these bottlenecks from the company's production process.

Yield: A 20 per cent rise in productivity led to the profitability of the dental product range increasing by 7.5 per cent.

### Vignette 2

Mary was a business development manager in a company producing videos.

Situation: The company's range of pop videos had been losing market share over several months.

Action: Mary identified a need to give the videos a more distinct marketing profile. She negotiated funding to use a top graphic design house to develop a new style of packaging for this range of products.

Yield: Sales increased by 1.5 per cent as the company's pop videos achieved a clearer identity.

Aim to produce at least 20 vignettes, some of which could relate to non-professional activities such as raising funds for your child's school or running a social club.

## Your database of skills, knowledge and experience

When you have completed the difficult but most important task of identifying your own achievements, the next stage in unpacking your kitbag is to conduct an in-depth audit of the skills, knowledge and experience that have contributed to these achievements. This process will raise your awareness of your own strengths and enable you to describe them confidently to others. More importantly at this stage, the skills audit will also help you identify those areas where you need to develop your competences further. The following case study illustrates this point.

---

### Case study: A deficit of diplomacy

Carlos, a talented young designer, appeared to have a rosy future in the fashion business. However, he failed to understand that his 'bulldozing' manner of getting things done did not fit in with his company's culture, which emphasised teamwork and co-operation. When he was passed over for promotion, he realized that he needed to learn and understand more about himself, and he asked one of the company's senior directors to help him do this.

Regular sessions with this mentor helped Carlos appreciate that while he was highly competent in the technical areas associated with his position, he had not developed his communication and inter-personal skills to the same level. This realization helped him modify his behaviour, particularly his abrasive style of communicating with colleagues and subordinates.

After six months of dedicated work Carlos began to fit in better with the team and understand how he needed to change his behaviour further if a senior position was to be his.

---

As the above case study demonstrates, open and positive communication with colleagues and clients is becoming more and more critical to career success.

### Activity 2: Your skills audit

Look back at the notes you made while tackling the first activity in this chapter. Consider the skills, knowledge and experience that contributed to the achievements you described in each of your vignettes.

List these under the following headings: verbal, numerical, inter-personal, creative, manual, problem-solving and technical skills.

Now make another list of the competences required in your current or most recent job, using the same headings.

Any mismatch between the two lists you have drawn up will help you identify those areas in which you need to develop further. On the other hand, a comparison between the two may also highlight competences which you are not exploiting as fully as you might be — which was what the character in the following case study discovered after carrying out a similar skills audit.

## Case study: Finding a new direction

Neil had started working in a large Midlands law practice shortly after qualifying as a solicitor. He had been identified as a 'high flier' early on and had progressed rapidly to become first a partner, and then a senior partner in the practice. He specialised in conveyancing, and by the age of 40 was in charge of a team of 10 clerks and junior solicitors.

When a slump in the housing market caused a marked fall in conveyancing business, Neil's partners proposed a reorgani-zation of his unit. He resisted this change which would have seen his responsibilities — and earnings — shrink considerably, but found himself outvoted by his partners. Stunned by this turn of events, he resigned.

Rather than drifting straight into another law practice, Neil enrolled on a programme of one-to-one career counselling to help him decide on his next move. As part of this programme, he looked at his successes and failures to date and carried out an in-depth skills audit. This process helped him appreciate that his main strength lay in his ability to think laterally and creatively — a strength which had not been fully exploited in his previous role in conveyancing.

Neil decided he'd had enough of legal practice and focused his job search on commercial organizations.

Three months later, he found a position in a rapidly expanding transportation company, which was able to put to good use both his legal expertise and his capacity for coming up with new ideas.

Like Neil in the above case study, you should find that developing a clear understanding of your own core skills and interests can help you move in a direction which meets your needs and values.

## *Activity 3: Assessing your interpersonal skills*

The last activity we asked you to carry out in this chapter should have helped you identify the skills and competences that contributed to your past successes. Many of these will probably have been the technical or functional skills associated with your educational and career background. Others will have been the interpersonal and self-management skills that are needed in all occupations. In this activity we will help you look in more detail at these 'soft' skills lurking in your kitbag.

First assess your own strength in each of the areas listed below by ticking the appropriate box.

| | Poor | Adequate | Good | Excellent |
|---|---|---|---|---|
| Communicating with colleagues | ❑ | ❑ | ❑ | ❑ |
| Communicating with bosses | ❑ | ❑ | ❑ | ❑ |
| Communicating with subordinates | ❑ | ❑ | ❑ | ❑ |
| Adapting to change | ❑ | ❑ | ❑ | ❑ |
| Handling chaos | ❑ | ❑ | ❑ | ❑ |
| Coping with pressure | ❑ | ❑ | ❑ | ❑ |
| Dealing with customers or clients | ❑ | ❑ | ❑ | ❑ |
| Taking risks | ❑ | ❑ | ❑ | ❑ |
| Taking initiative | ❑ | ❑ | ❑ | ❑ |
| Seeking out opportunities | ❑ | ❑ | ❑ | ❑ |
| Demonstrating self-confidence | ❑ | ❑ | ❑ | ❑ |
| Organizing your own work | ❑ | ❑ | ❑ | ❑ |
| Monitoring own activities | ❑ | ❑ | ❑ | ❑ |
| Analysing problems | ❑ | ❑ | ❑ | ❑ |
| Making timely decisions | ❑ | ❑ | ❑ | ❑ |
| Meeting deadlines | ❑ | ❑ | ❑ | ❑ |
| Working with others | ❑ | ❑ | ❑ | ❑ |
| Delegating to others | ❑ | ❑ | ❑ | ❑ |
| Giving honest feedback | ❑ | ❑ | ❑ | ❑ |
| Adapting behaviour to different situations | ❑ | ❑ | ❑ | ❑ |

The second part of this activity is more open-ended — and time-consuming! Write a paragraph describing how you have demonstrated competence in each of the areas where you have rated your performance as 'excellent' or 'good'. For example, if you pride yourself on your ability to organise your own work, you might describe a particular project you have managed.

Do the same with the areas in which you consider your competence 'poor' or merely 'adequate'. If, for example, you know you are not very good at meeting deadlines, describe a situation in which this weakness manifested itself and consider how you might have handled the situation more effectively.

## Soft skills and hard decisions

We have asked you to spend a considerable amount of time identifying your communication, interpersonal and self-management skills, because, as we shall see in Chapter 10, it is these skills above all others, which will determine whether you achieve the future you want. This is not to say, of course, that technical and functional skills are not important. They are, particularly if you are at an early stage of your career. But the danger of being seen purely as a functional specialist is that you will always be asked to do the same kind of job and never gain the wide experience that is the key to survival and success in today's uncertain world.

Many specialists and functional line managers reach a 'plateau' in their 30s because they do not appreciate the importance of communication and other 'soft' skills. They fail to understand and manage relationships, to get the best out of others and to let people know — without appearing conceited — of their own achievements. Consequently they are left behind.

Later chapters in this book will help you develop your competence in some of these soft skill areas. But for now it is important to remember that communication involves listening to yourself as well as to others. Beginning to understand your own achievements will give you confidence and help you identify your own needs and concerns. As you have probably found while working through the activities in this chapter, this is not an easy process but it is one that provides an essential foundation for success.

# Where are you going?

## Mapping a career path

Earlier in this book we touched on the economic changes that have led to the dismantling of traditional corporate hierarchies and the erosion of job security. These profound changes in the nature of employment will influence the direction your own career is likely to take in the years to come.

Few people in the world's advanced economies can now predict with any confidence where they will be working or what they will be doing in five years' time or even if their current employer will still exist at that point. Since the certainties that earlier generations took for granted have disappeared, individuals must now take responsibility for their own professional growth. You may find this a daunting prospect if in the past you have relied on your boss or a paternalistic personnel department to plan and manage your career path. But an understanding of how the world of work has changed can make this task more manageable.

The very concept of a 'career' is undergoing a transformation as companies 'downsize' and outsource an increasing number of functions. With the prospects for climbing a career ladder steadily diminishing, the rung on which you find yourself at any one point becomes an even less appropriate symbol of professional growth and achievement than it was in the past. It is now more helpful to think in terms of career 'lattices' — crisscross frameworks that support moves in all directions. Success no longer lies in acquiring ever more impressive-sounding job titles but in the quality of the contribution you make and of your collaboration with others.

For most people the adjustment to this new reality requires a radical re-evaluation of long-held attitudes and values. This was the experience of the high-flying executive who is the subject of our next case study.

### Case study: Lateral moves

Michael held a senior general management position in the Scottish division of a large UK retailing concern which he had joined 20 years earlier as a graduate trainee. He had hoped to remain with the company for the rest of his working life and continue his steady rise to the top. When the company was sold off to an American group which brought in its own top team, however, Michael was obliged to start looking for another job.

For many months he focused his search on the retail sector, applying only for general management positions at a level he considered appropriate to his previous experience and seniority. When these applications failed to yield a single interview, he finally began looking at other employment sectors. This approach proved more productive, but when Michael was eventually offered a job — as deputy finance director in a manufacturing group — he turned it down as being too junior. Despite all the well-documented changes in the nature of employment, he still viewed the world of work in hierarchical terms.

It was not until a year later that he began to consider an alternative to continued progression on a vertical career path. Using what remained of his severance package, he set up as an independent consultant, and was immediately offered a short-term contract managing a project for his former company. Though at first he found it difficult to adjust to his new role outside the company's hierarchy, this initial assignment led to others as he re-established old contacts and began to forge new ones. As his values and assumptions changed, he was able to build up a thriving consultancy business.

Like Michael in this case study, you too will need to look at career growth in diverse and creative ways. Expanding your role and taking on new projects in different areas can be important elements of this process.

## Rethinking attitudes and assumptions

In a world where there is no job security but plenty of work you can begin developing the attitudes needed for successful career planning by asking yourself the following question:

What do I need to learn so that I can decide what to do next?

This is a significant departure from asking yourself:

How can I prepare for the next promotion?

The first question is based on the positive assumption that you need to take responsibility for your own personal and professional growth. Searching for an answer to this question may lead you to embark on a formal programme of training and development. But it could also help you acquire the mind-set needed to take on a series of projects or assignments that are right for you at each stage of your development.

These assignments need not necessarily be in different organizations. Many graduates start their careers in large organizations because they have not yet worked out where to place themselves and because these organizations send recruiters to university campuses. Even if you are working in one of these corporations, however, you must make decisions about your own future because no one is going to make them for you. In the past these decisions might have revolved around the question of when to put in for the next promotion; today, cross-functional, sideways moves have become more important, with a switch from marketing to accounting, for example, likely to do more for your career than promotion from the post of marketing manager to that of deputy marketing director. In other words, the most effective way of enhancing your employability both with current and prospective employers is to build up a portfolio of wide-ranging experiences and skills.

If you are to develop such a portfolio, you must be clear about how you are contributing to your organization at the moment and what your contribution might be, say, within the next two years. If you are not currently in paid employment, you will need to think about the contribution you made to organizations you worked for in the past and what you might be able to do for those that employ you in the future. You then have to make sure that others know about this contribution — whether they are prospective employers or the people you now work with and report to. As we shall see in a later chapter in this book, self-promotion is central to the successful management of any career.

## Activity 1: Evaluating your contribution

Use the following checklist to assess the quality of your contribution to your present — or most recent — organization, whether you worked there in a full-time, part-time, temporary, permanent or even voluntary capacity. If you are an independent consultant, consider one of your recent assignments.

■  I am making the most of my current position.

■  I do more than the minimum expected of me.

■ I look for opportunities to do extra work.

■ When I spot problems I look for solutions.

■ I look for ways of improving existing systems.

■ I have ideas about how the organization's products or services might be improved.

■ I let other people know my ideas.

■ I seek feedback from others about my ideas.

■ I respond to feedback in order to improve my ideas.

■ I keep myself informed about the organization's plans.

■ When I approach the end of a task or project I plan what I want to work on next.

## Dreaming of the future

We all have dreams and visions of what we would really like to be and do. These are important because unless you set yourself a standard for what you want to achieve and learn, you are likely to settle for an existence that is second best. In other words, you must identify your goals and imagine what it is like to achieve them. Planning will then help you work out what you need to do to achieve those goals.

### *Activity 2: Turning dreams into reality*

To set out on this planning process, you need first to suspend your critical faculties and allow yourself to dream. If there were no obstacles in the way, what would you most like to be, to do and to have? Let your mind range freely over the possibilities in all areas of your life — career, finance, personal and social life, mental and physical fitness. Make a list of these dreams or goals and compare it with the list you drew up for Activity 5 in Chapter 2.

Some of the dreams on your list will probably be unattainable. An adult measuring five feet six inches will never be six feet tall! So discard dreams of this kind and stick to those which are both challenging and realistic. Now sort out the remaining items on your list into short, medium and long-term goals — defining the latter as those likely to take three to five years to attain. Remember that what is a short-term goal for one person may only be attainable in the long-term for someone else. If, for example, you want to speak French fluently, it will take you far longer to reach this goal if you are a complete novice than it would if you have already studied the language at school.

The next step in this activity is to relate the goals on your list to the different areas that make up your life. Use the following example as a guide.

## Goal list

### Career
- Gain experience in a different function/department (short-term)
- Enrol on an MBA programme (medium-term)
- Move to a different organization (medium-term)
- Become managing director (long-term)

### Finance
- Pay off overdraft (short-term)
- Increase earnings by 10-12 per cent (medium-term)
- Pay off mortgage (long-term)
- Earn £50,000+ a year (long term)

### Personal and social life
- Go out more often (short-term)
- Look up old school/college friends (short-term)
- Learn how to ski (medium-term)
- Start a family (long-term)

### Mental well being
- Stop putting off difficult decisions (short-term)
- Learn to relax (medium-term)
- Become a more tolerant, positive person (long-term)
- Avoid working excessively long hours (short-term)

### Health and physical well being
- Stop smoking (short-term)
- Lose 14 lbs (medium-term)
- Become fit enough to run the London Marathon (long-term)

When you have categorized your goals, you will be in a position to start thinking about how to attain them. This involves setting yourself a number of small, intermediate goals. To go back to our earlier example, if one of your long-term goals is to speak French fluently, your first step will be to enrol in a beginner's class with the aim of acquiring a basic, 'survival' level knowledge of the language in, say, six months and reaching GCSE level in a couple of years. The next step may involve joining an advanced class, followed by total immersion in the language — perhaps by spending several weeks in a French-speaking country. Each of these steps will have taken you closer to your final goal of fluency in French.

Plan how you will achieve your own goals by making copies of the following form and filling it in for each of the most important goals on your original list.

**GOAL:**


**AREA: (career, finance etc.)**


**TIME SCALE FOR ACHIEVING GOAL:**


**SKILLS AND ATTRIBUTES NEEDED TO ACHIEVE IT:**


**WHERE AM I NOW IN RELATION TO THIS GOAL?**


**INTERMEDIATE STEPS:**                     **DEADLINES:**

1.

2.

3.

4.

5.

## Beliefs and values

The goals you set yourself in your personal and professional life inevitably reflect your individual beliefs and values. Values are those things that matter most to you, be they emotional states, personal attributes or material possessions. They exercise a magnetic pull over the direction of your life and it is therefore crucial that you understand what they are. For example, if you value leading others, then you should aim to achieve a leadership role. On the other hand, if you place little value on 'empowering' others, do not strive for a management role requiring a high level of people management skills, but focus instead on securing a position in which other kinds of skills play an important part.

The dangers inherent in losing touch with your own values are illustrated by the following case study.

### Case study: Keeping in touch

James had joined a major financial services company straight after leaving school. He had no formal qualifications but his evident intelligence, diligence and, above all, ability to work with others soon came to the notice of the company's management. He gained rapid promotion, studied in the evenings for a degree and by his late thirties had become the company's financial controller. He was respected by his fellow managers and had a reputation for getting the best out of his subordinates.

But when James was appointed managing director of one of the company's subsidiaries, he seemed to change. He viewed his new role with some trepidation and this lack of confidence soon led him to adopt an autocratic, 'like it or lump it' attitude. His team found it difficult to communicate with him, he became more and more isolated, and business performance began to suffer.

Formerly very much a team player, James eventually came to recognise that his behaviour as MD clashed with his basic belief in the importance of teamwork. This new understanding of the need to keep in touch with his own values enabled him to start modifying his behaviour and he is now more like his old self.

As this case study demonstrates, it is extremely important for you to recognise when your value system may be in conflict with the way you are behaving at work. Insist to yourself that you maintain a comfortable harmony between the two!

## *Activity 3: Getting in touch with your own values*

Find out what your current values are by listing the things you value most in life and then ranking them in order of importance. Here are some examples to help get you started.

| | |
|---|---|
| ■ happiness | ■ creativity |
| ■ power | ■ recognition |
| ■ community | ■ helpfulness |
| ■ health | ■ loyalty |
| ■ altruism | ■ integrity |
| ■ security | ■ competition |
| ■ freedom | ■ affection |
| ■ wealth | ■ adventure |
| ■ success | ■ risk |
| ■ friendship | ■ pleasure |

The items on your list and the order in which you rank them will say a great deal about the kind of person you are and why you tend to head in certain directions and not in others. But this simple activity may also reveal why there may be times when you are pulled in different directions. If, for example, your top two priorities are 'power' and 'friendship', there is probably a great deal of conflict in your life since your desire to have power over people is likely to prevent you from forming close friendships. Thinking about your values and identifying conflicts between them will help you rearrange your priorities.

## Goals and values

Your career success will to a large extent depend on how closely you align your career goals with your personal values. Although you may be able to reorder some of your priorities, your basic values were determined at an early age and will be difficult to change. If you value loyalty, therefore, you are unlikely to succeed in reaching a senior position in an organization with a dog-eat-dog culture! Similarly, if in the last activity you placed 'freedom' high on your list of values, you will not be happy or successful in a role in which your activities will be subject to close supervision. So now that you have identified both your goals and your values, your next step is to check how well they match each other. The following activity is designed to help you do that.

## Activity 4: Aligning goals and values

Consider how closely your current situation is aligned to your values and beliefs by writing a short paragraph in answer to each of the following questions. If any of your answers reveal discontent with an aspect of your life, try to analyse exactly what it is that is causing that discontent. On the other hand, if you answer any of these questions in the affirmative, try to identify and describe the elements of your situation that give rise to positive feelings.

■ Are you content with your present lifestyle?

■ Are you content with your achievements to date?

■ Do you feel you have control over your own future?

■ Do your goals have the support of the people to whom you feel closest?

■ Are you able to defend your own interests without undermining those of the organization you work for?

■ Do you manage to remain loyal to yourself without undermining others?

■ Do you share the values of your organization (or boss)?

The following case study highlights the tensions that can arise when individuals find their own values at odds with those of their employers.

## Case study: A clash of values

Patricia, the only child of a skilled craftsman and a mother who did not work outside the home, had a caring, traditional upbringing. Her parents were involved in local affairs and were respected members of their community. A bright student, Patricia won a scholarship to the best grammar school in the area, went to university and eventually completed a PhD in chemistry.

She could have become an academic but chose instead to join a small but highly respected company specializing in the production of paint and protective coatings. Patricia flourished in this environment and at the age of 40 became head of the firm's research laboratory.

The firm was family-owned and had always invested in long-term research and development. Its products were known throughout the world for their durability and resistance to corrosion. But a new generation of family members was less involved in the business and pressure grew to sell it to a large international chemical and paint company. Patricia was now a board member but could not prevent the sale going through, hard though she tried.

The new management assured her that her position would not be affected by the change of ownership and that the small research group she headed would continue to function. Within a few months, however, her group was absorbed into the central laboratories and Patricia herself 'demoted' to the position of assistant director of research. Pressure grew to abandon long-term research in favour of short-term profit. The final straw for Patricia was a marketing decision to downgrade those product lines on which the company's world-wide reputation had rested: the original small company name still featured on these products but their quality was inferior.

Patricia had always valued quality and integrity and felt she was compromising these values by remaining with the company. Her position finally became untenable when she told a reporter for a trade magazine what was happening!

Soon after resigning, Patricia was able to use her contacts in the industry to find a position as head of a joint venture between a research institute and another small manufacturer of protective coatings. Now she was once more working in an organization whose values were the same as her own.

Patricia's story demonstrates that it is important for you to understand your own value system and ensure you feel at ease with the values of organizations you are working in or with.

## *Activity 5: Drawing up a career plan*

Examine the role that you ultimately wish to pursue, and consider whether it is realistically aligned with the values and attitudes you identified while working through this chapter. If, for example, you put a premium on freedom and creativity, you may need to think twice before looking for a role in an environment that demands a high degree of conformity from those who work in it. Now list your strengths and the areas which you need to develop further if you are to attain your career goal. Remember, we all need to pay constant attention to managing our time and relationships and to communicating in an open, clear and positive manner.

Finally, develop a detailed plan — with intermediate steps — to help you attain your goal. Make sure you include deadlines for achieving each of these intermediate goals as well as a deadline for your ultimate goal. Consider also how your plan is likely to fit in with your personal circumstances and needs. Read and reflect on all the work you have done so far before starting this activity.

# Repack your Kitbag

## What do you need in your kitbag?

By now you have started forming a picture of where you want to get to and how you plan to reach that destination. The next stage is to decide what skills you need for this journey and what you need to do to develop them. While Chapter 4 should have helped you recognize the skills you already have, the emphasis here is on identifying skills areas which may need further development.

First, though, let us think about learning. We take the position that learning is a continuous and lifelong activity — *éducation permanente*, as the French call it. Some of this learning takes place in formal situations — in school or on training courses — but most takes place in the course of everyday living. This everyday learning is sometimes deliberate and conscious, but much of it is unconscious or accidental, and it is often only when a need arises that you realize what you have already learnt.

If you are to achieve the future that you want, you need to develop the ability to learn effectively. This is not simply a case of learning how to pass courses and examinations such as the MBA, but of seeing every moment as an opportunity to learn. For example, if you are delayed at an airport or a railway station and you find that you have nothing to do — nothing to read or to work on — what do you do? Many people will become irritated in this type of situation, while others will perhaps be lucky enough to be able to catch up on their sleep. But an unexpected delay can also present an opportunity to learn. Next time you find yourself with time on your hands in a public place, try out the following activities.

1.  Study the advertisements displayed on the walls around you. What are they saying? How successful are they in conveying their messages? Why have the advertisers chosen certain methods of presentation in preference to others?

2.  Watch people as they meet and greet each other, as they sit and read, and as they look around at you. What do their behaviour, demeanour and dress tell you about them?

3.   You could even strike up a conversation! As a further training exercise see if you can avoid getting into the routine of moaning about that train cancellation or delayed flight.

These activities will help you develop the skills of observing, thinking and communicating, and will be a better use of your time than allowing yourself to become upset over the delay. They also serve to illustrate our fundamental position that effectiveness in life depends on an open and observing mind that continually notices, analyses and revises its views, always adding to its store of experience.

## How learning takes place

We are not going to explore learning in terms of the biological or physical processes involved, but rather in logical and descriptive terms.

Consider the following sequence of events which illustrates how learning takes place.

1.   You are at a meeting which is not going particularly well. The person running the meeting suggests a pause while all those present write down two ideas for moving things forward. When these ideas are shared around the table, there is a striking similarity between them; the meeting is re-energized and ends with an excellent plan for action.

2.   You think about this event and reflect on how it seemed to change the behaviour of those present.

3.   You review how you have run meetings in the past and decide that you will make some changes in your style.

4.   At the next meeting you run, you pay more attention to the climate of the meeting, you summarize more effectively and you use the device of a two-minutes silence to give members a chance to think and come up with their own ideas.

5.   This subsequent meeting constitutes a further learning event, enabling you to observe and review once more your strategy for running effective meetings.

Simple as all this may sound, you have just revised your theory of
running meetings and altered your behaviour as a result. In other
words, you have learnt something!

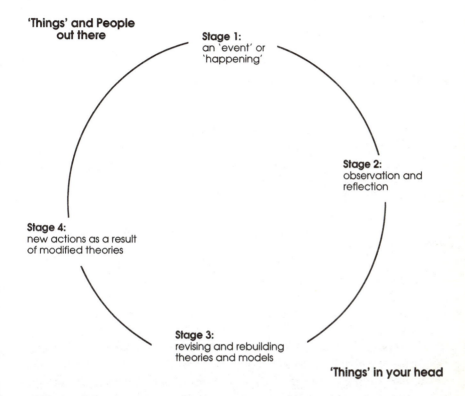

**Figure 6.1**  *The learning cycle*

All learning follows this cycle*. Stages 1 and 4 take place 'out there',
while stages 2 and 3 take place in your head. Though learning cannot
occur unless we go through all four stages, too often we behave as if
we have short-circuited this cycle. For example, under pressure, we
sometimes rush from the 'event' that constitutes stage 1 straight to an
action, without stopping to consider all the options. Alternatively,
faced with a difficult decision we sometimes become paralyzed as we
mull over what we already know instead of seeking more information
on which to base the decision.

   To maximize your effectiveness as a learner, you need to improve
your ability to move through all stages of the cycle. Too often we let
events pass by without sufficient concern or attention, missing the
opportunity to reflect and learn as we go.

---

* This was first pointed out by David Kolb and further developed by Peter Honey (see Further
Reading on page 150).

## Improving your learning skills

Associated with the learning cycle, there are three main sets of skills which are crucial to success in whatever role or job you have or hope to have. These are:

1.   Skills that enable you to observe and acquire information.

2.   Skills that enable you to analyse, process and draw conclusions from that information.

3.   Skills that enable you to take action to test out and implement your conclusions. In the rest of this chapter we shall consider each of these sets of skills in turn and provide suggestions for your further development.

## Observing and acquiring information

The skills of observing and acquiring information are required at stages 1 and 2 of the learning cycle. They enable you to notice, to observe, to sense and to acquire information. But before we can consider these skills in detail, we need to consider the problem of perception.

We are always trying to 'make sense' of what is going on around us. Since so much of this is potentially confusing, the brain often simplifies, modifies or simply represses what is happening. Often this filtering process takes place as events unfold before our eyes and ears — a phenomenon demonstrated by the Viennese professor who, early in this century, staged a 'happening' in one of his lectures. In order to demonstrate the unreliability of witnesses to crimes, he had arranged for a woman — naked underneath her coat — to dart into the lecture theatre. A man followed, a shot was fired and the two of them rushed out through a door behind the lecturer. Not surprisingly, the professor collected many different accounts of what had taken place a few moments earlier in front of everyone's eyes.

Because of this filtering process we are not even aware of much of what goes on around us. To verify this you have only to remember a time when you were deeply engrossed in a task and oblivious to things and people around you that in other circumstances would have been intrusive or irritating.

Selective perception is not necessarily a bad thing. It is, in fact, essential to sanity! Without it every noise, every movement, every sight would be registered consciously and you would be paralyzed. The act of walking along a busy street would become both impossible and unsafe if you consciously processed every signal you received as you walked. However, selective perception can become a hindrance in situations requiring full attention. 'Automatic' processing is also unlikely to lead to the most appropriate responses when new thinking or a fresh outlook is needed.

## Looking and listening

Let us pause for a moment. Listening and looking are the two modes through which we acquire most of the information that we need in order to learn. We know a great deal about these basic skills. We know that, unless special efforts are made, our ability to retain much of what passes through our senses is severely limited. Yet we still do little to ensure that, when we need to, we do remember what we have seen or heard.

## Looking

Quite simply, this is the ability to use your eyes to see all that is happening around you — to notice things and people, to see events and to observe them. Aim to improve your powers of observation through practice, and use every opportunity to do so. Help yourself by taking notes, by occasionally staying silent in meetings, by watching TV with the sound turned down and by testing your capacity to look and record in any other way you can.

## Listening

Listen to a news bulletin on the radio or TV. Just before the next bulletin an hour later, jot down the main items you remember from the earlier bulletin. Unless you make a special effort you will probably find you have difficulty remembering more than two or three items out of perhaps a dozen. But against all the evidence, we still tend to rely too much on our ears alone. Watch the people at the next meeting you attend: how many of them are taking notes? Yet if they are not, what is the value of the meeting to them? The evidence is that, typically, we retain only around 25 per cent of what we hear in day-to-day conversation unless we make a particular effort to retain more of that information.

The only way to increase your powers of observation is to 'practise' as you go through each day. For example, when you make a purchase in a shop, ask yourself as you walk out of the door what you can recall about the scene you have just left. What do you remember about the sales assistant, other customers, the cash till, the counter? Make a note of your recollections. Similarly, if you have just been to a meeting in a room that was new to you, try to recall what it looked like, how many chairs there were, what pictures were hanging on the walls and so on. Again, write down what you are able to recall.

You may say that the appearance of a room is unimportant, but it is only by developing a sharp awareness of your surroundings that you will be able to improve your listening and looking skills. You will then be able to observe and remember what *is* of crucial importance to you. In other words we are not talking here about 'memory tricks' but about sensible day-to-day observation which will improve your ability to learn from and manage a whole range of situations.

## Activity 1: Increasing your powers of observation

Aim in the course of the next week to pause three times each day to record what you have been doing in the previous thirty minutes. Make a note of:

■   who you were with

■   what you said or did

■   what other people present said or did

■   what they were wearing

■   what your surroundings looked like.

## Activity 2: Your daily journal

The purpose of this activity is two-fold. By keeping a journal of what happens to you each day you will continue to sharpen your powers of perception. The process of recording the highs and lows of each day will also help you recall key events and your feelings about them. Such observations will serve as an important aid to the management and development of your career.

You should record:

■   important events and decisions

■ your reactions to these events and decisions, and your feelings — both positive and negative — about them

■ your impressions of other people and their behaviour

■ your feelings about things you did not achieve

■ what you think you could do differently in the future.

It seems to us no accident that many successful people from all walks of life have made it a habit to record their lives in diaries. Apart from the value these diaries may have for historians or biographers, we believe that the reflection that *has* to take place whenever experiences are recorded ensured that the individuals concerned learnt from those experiences.

## Acquiring information from other people

Much of the information we need in life is in the heads of other people, and we acquire this information by questioning them. Asking questions effectively requires a clear idea of what you want to find out, or at least the ability to recognize when your questions are taking you in a useful direction. Some kinds of questions tend to open up areas of information or investigation, while other types of questions tend to narrow the scope for further investigation. Conversations are usually a mixture of both types of question, together with statements of what we know or want.

Often we tend to use too many 'closing down' questions which are actually disguised instructions or opinions — for example: 'Don't you think it would be a good idea if...?' Particularly in the early stages of any conversation or investigation we should aim to ask open questions such as: 'Tell me about...' or 'How do you think we could...?'

Open questions encourage people to talk, to open up, to make suggestions, and you learn more if you use such questions. On the other hand, there will be situations where you may find that focused questions are more productive. If someone is giving a confused or complicated account of a situation, then questions such as: 'What exactly happened?' or 'What specifically are you trying to achieve?' may help clarify things.

Every day offers you countless opportunities to develop your questioning skills. To exploit these opportunities, resist the temptation to direct conversations until you are sure that it will be helpful to do so. Monitor yourself so that you can detect when the questions you are about to ask are, in effect, commands, statements or attempts to put words into other people's mouths. Finally, in all conversations, you need to look as well as listen. Facial expression and body language convey much of a speaker's message and, in particular, give clues to that person's comfort and emotions.

## Acquiring information from reading and research

Successful people are usually well informed, not only about developments in their own field but also more generally. One of the reasons they are able to network successfully is that they can talk about subjects of interest to a wide range of people. As we shall see in the next chapter, networking is one of the most important of all career management tools. You should therefore widen your own horizons by reading fiction, poetry, biography and other categories of books, as well as books and articles about your own field. It is also a good idea to read at least one newspaper a day. To paraphrase an advertising slogan used by one national newspaper: unless you read regularly you will have no comment to make on many of the events that shape our lives.

Unlike watching TV, which is often passive and unplanned, reading is an active occupation. You will find that the more you read, the easier it will become to assimilate complex information quickly. This has always been an important skill for those in technical, managerial or professional roles, but in today's information-based economy it has become even more crucial.

### Research skills

Here people with a science or engineering background may have the edge over others, but anyone can develop research skills through practice. These skills include:

■ formulating objectives or hypotheses

■ constructing plans for research and action

■ collecting relevant data and observations

■ asking relevant questions of other people

■ using the information collected to develop solutions and determine courses of action

■ evaluating outcomes against the original objectives

■ formulating further plans in the light of the outcomes. Career management is, in effect, the application of the above research model to your own life and career — an iterative process which involves regular evaluation of current outcomes against original and evolving intentions.

## Activity 3: Harnessing information relevant to your career

For this exercise you will need to spend a few hours in a library with a good business reference section. The aim is not to read everything but to identify sources of information relevant to your career or business and so ensure that when you need information, you know where and how to go about finding it.
Make a note of:

■ directories that contain information about organizations, whether companies or other types of organizations such as charities, committees, associations

■ directories that relate to specific sectors or industries, such as advertising, oil, education

■ directories that contain references to other published information, such as books, magazines, newspapers, journals and other directories.

You will find that many directories are now available on CD-ROM in the better libraries.

It has been our observation that many managers and professionals are ill-equipped in these basic skills of using information sources. This is all too obvious when they are faced with a major challenge such as redundancy. Many individuals show that they have little idea of how to go about finding information relevant to their job search. Like any other major project or business activity, this has to be tackled in a systematic and informed way.

## Self measuring and monitoring

Measuring and monitoring are particular forms of listening and looking which enable you to estimate how close you are to meeting an aim or objective. Depending on the activity concerned, measurement may be easy — as in the case of salary for work done — or difficult — as in the case of how others perceive you. In later chapters we discuss how you should go about seeking and receiving feedback from those you work with and for. But for successful career management, the ability to assess your own progress against predetermined goals is also essential, and this includes monitoring and reading signals that may be at variance with the words they accompany.

By carefully monitoring your environment, you will be able to avoid becoming engrossed in work or tasks that are no longer as relevant or important as they were, and to appreciate if other people's views about you have changed.

### Case study: Misreading the signals

Basil's role in a music publishing company was to analyse market trends. A quiet, conscientious worker with an analytical mind, he was good at producing detailed reports. What he did not notice was that the company's marketing team rarely acted on his recommendations. He was therefore surprised when the company decided to outsource the work he had been doing.

Had Basil been less engrossed in the detail of his work, and more alert to the warning signals, he might have been able to refocus his activities and so protect his job.

It is important that you take stock of your situation at regular intervals and keep a dialogue with yourself alive. That way, you will not fall into the same trap as the character in the above case study, and lose sight of what is happening around you.

## Summary: Observing and acquiring information

We have spent some time on these skills since, in our experience, they are often ignored or assumed to be well developed in mature adults.

However, as we have seen, it is not difficult to find evidence to the contrary. In an increasingly uncertain and unpredictable future, the ability to observe accurately and acquire information will be more relevant than ever.

## Analysing and processing information

Having observed and recorded information, you need to be able to use it appropriately and effectively. The skills involved in this process fall into two main groups:

■ the skills of analysis, review, revision and evaluation

■ the skills of developing and creating ideas, solutions and proposals for action.

Taken together, these skills comprise what are usually called 'thinking and problem-solving'. Unlike the skills of observing and acquiring information, these skills have received a considerable amount of attention from management educators. Since there are plenty of readily available books and courses on thinking and problem-solving skills, we do not intend to cover them in any detail here. We urge you to consult the reading list on page 150 for suitable books, and if you do have the opportunity to attend a course covering this area, take it.

That said, we now provide a general guide to problem-solving which can be applied to any problem, however small or complex.

Most real-life problems are complex, involving many factors and influences. To solve such problems you need to be able to break them down into sub-problems and examine each one until you find a solution. Clear, logical thinking is essential, together with the complementary skills of flexible and creative thinking. The trouble is that most of us have not been taught to think either creatively or logically.

### Blocks to clear thought

We are all surrounded by attempts by advertisers, the media, politicians and others to manipulate our thinking. Understanding illogical thinking in yourself and in others will enable you to resist these attempts, while also helping you in your problem-solving.

The main barriers to clear thought are:

■ the tendency to generalize from one example or the most recent occurrence

■ arguments which appeal to emotion or to the 'greater good'

■ stereotypical thinking about situations or people

■ poor or insufficient data, errors of fact, misuse of statistics

■ assuming cause and effect simply because two events occur closely in time

■ misunderstanding caused by poor communication

■ allowing pressure to lead to hasty conclusions based on hunches

■ assuming that old methods and answers will work in new situations.

## Activity 4: Faulty thinking

Think back over decisions you have made or situations where you have been involved in problem-solving. These could be either personal or work related.

Identify examples of the above barriers to logical thinking. If you are honest with yourself you will find that almost every decision you have made will have featured some of these barriers.

In making many day-to-day decisions — for example, about what film to see at the weekend — the quality of our thinking does not really matter. But for career decisions, logical thinking is clearly crucial.

Assume that you are thinking about changing jobs or making some other career move. Make some notes on how you might overcome some of the above barriers to logical thinking listed above.

## A systematic approach

A systematic approach will help you tackle complex problems in a logical way. The essential steps are listed below:

**Step 1**    **Clarify the goal**

What do I want to achieve?
What prevents me from achieving it?
What will 'success' look like?
What is *my* problem? (as opposed to someone else's)
Why do I want to achieve it?

**Step 2**    **Collect information**

Where am I now?
What else do I need to know?
Who has relevant information?
How do I go about collecting it?
How do I keep biases and stereotypes out of it?

**Step 3**    **Analyse and classify information**

What does all this information mean?
How can I classify and organize it?
What connections are there between different bits of it?
Is anything missing? If so, what is it and how can I find it?
Does the information alter my perception of the problem? If so, do I need to reformulate my goals?

**Step 4**    **Develop solutions**

What is the ideal solution?
What criteria can I use to assess possible solutions?
What will success look and feel like?
How will I know when I am on the road to being successful?

**Step 5**    **Choose solutions**

Check against criteria developed in Step 4

Consider:
- time
- cost
- practicality
- probability of success

■    seriousness of failure
■    contingency plans if solution does not work.

List 'fors' and 'againsts' and use weighting procedures to
check out options.

### Step 6    Implementation

Who is involved?
What are the attitudes for or against change?
What communication style is appropriate?
What areas are open for discussion or negotiation?
How will I monitor outcomes?
Do I have contingency plans or a fallback position?

### Step 7    Evaluation

How is my solution working out?
If it has not worked, why not?
Implement contingency plans and/or go back to earlier
steps.

All real-life problem-solving is likely to involve recycling, jumping
stages or responding to unpredicted or changed circumstances, so
the above seven-step process is not intended to be followed rigidly.
But it does provide a framework to enable you to judge where you are
at any stage of tackling a problem. It also provides a much-needed
structure that helps counter natural tendencies to rush at solutions,
to play hunches, to back off obstacles or to narrow the field of
investigation too soon.

## Developing your creativity

One of the biggest blocks to creativity is the widely-held belief that it
is a rare attribute, possessed only by those individuals known to be
the original thinkers in their chosen field. This is a narrow definition
of creativity which only serves to make most people think they are not
creative. In fact, we can all develop an ability to think creatively.

Creative thinking is thinking which provides new ways of looking
at problems. We do it all the time in that any problem which does not
have an obvious solution has to be approached creatively. A new idea

has been defined as a combination of two or more known ideas — test any new idea against this and you will see that it works. The walkman, the hovercraft, the supermarket all fit this analysis.

Developing your powers of creative thinking is not so much an activity as the continuous application of a questioning attitude to all that you do. The opposite is linear extrapolation of the past into the future, and anything you can do to free yourself from such rigid behaviour will prepare you for those situations in which it is *essential* to think creatively. There is a direct link here to those basic skills of listening and questioning that we looked at earlier in this chapter. Many potentially valuable thoughts can be stifled by 'closing down' a discussion or an internal debate too soon.

Make sure you have a notebook — or a section in your diary — where you can capture ideas and thoughts as they occur to you. Students of art and design always carry notebooks in which they make sketches and stick cuttings. You would be wise to follow their example, since creativity needs feeding!

## Deciding on a direction

When you have analysed and processed information, and come up with ideas for action, you need to decide what to do. If you have carried out the earlier stages of problem-solving thoroughly, making decisions should be easy, if not automatic. In other words, if you have set yourself clear objectives to begin with, then the choice should follow on logically; if you have not, then making a decision may well be the hardest part — and indicate that you need to do more work on your aims and objectives.

Deciding usually means choosing between several possible courses of action, and requires:

■ a systematic way of evaluating options against objectives and

■ the courage to make the decision.

All decisions are, in the final analysis, emotional in that they require the exercise of judgement. A decision is only actually needed when the information available is less than perfect. For example, you do not need to make a decision as such about replacing a failed light bulb, though you do need to decide what type of bulb to use. Some methods to help you make decisions are listed below:

## 1.  Flip a coin

If you have several equally attractive alternatives this method may well work. It will certainly enable you to get on with the implementation of your solution!

## 2.  Arguing your case

With this method you imagine that you have to persuade a critical observer of the validity of each option, and write down the case for each one. As you do this you may find that one option stands out while the others are hard to justify.

## 3.  Balaam's ass

The ass in the fable starved because it stood halfway between two equally attractive bales of hay and could not decide which to choose. If you use this method, try to argue against each option so as to make it unattractive. One option may emerge unscathed from this process, though you may, of course, succeed in knocking them all down — in which case you need to revisit earlier stages in the problem-solving process.

## 4.  Ideal solution

Consider the ideal solution and describe its characteristics. Then compare each of the options to see which comes closest to that ideal.

## 5.  Balance sheet

List the plusses and minuses of each option in separate columns.

## 6.  Matrices

For important decisions, the evaluation methods outlined above may not be sufficiently detailed. An alternative is the matrix, which, in the case of a decision concerning a job change might look like this:

| Options | | | | |
|---|---|---|---|---|
| Deciding factors | Stay | Move company | Retrain | Other |
| Salary | | | | |
| Location | | | | |
| Prospects | | | | |
| Opportunities | | | | |
| Culture | | | | |
| Enjoyment | | | | |
| Values | | | | |
| Development opportunities | | | | |
| Use of skills | | | | |
| Interest | | | | |
| Satisfaction | | | | |

You can use words, ticks and crosses or a numerical weighting system to fill in the columns on the right.

There are, of course, more complex methods of evaluating technical or financial decisions but the above methods should suffice for most personal and career decisions. You may find after using one of these that you still dislike the outcome — in which case the process of weighing up different options will have served to uncover other factors that you may not have recognized as important or which you weighted insufficiently. Or it may have helped you face up to the reality of the situation — the car you already have will have to serve for a few years yet!

## Activity 5: Weighing up a career decision

Consider any decision related to your career. It could be something as radical as a complete change of direction or as routine as the decision whether or not to go on a short course. Use one of the methods outlined above to weigh up the available options.

### Skills for implementing decisions and taking action

Under this heading fall many of the traditional management skills: directing, proposing, negotiating, instructing, presenting, communicating and so on. Each in itself could form the subject of a training course or chapter in a management textbook, so in this chapter we intend to focus only on the core skill of using your time, and that of others, efficiently — a skill that is crucial to effectiveness in anything you may be doing. Later on we shall look at some of the other key management skills in the context of developing your career.

## Managing time

Time is one of your most valuable resources and it is under your own control. With today's lean organizations employing fewer people for longer hours than ever before, managing time has never been more important. If you are always rushing around, constantly juggling several tasks and never quite finishing any of them to your own satisfaction, then you are probably failing to manage your time effectively. In our experience those people who seem to be achieving whatever it is they want to achieve are also managing their time effectively!

The reasons why so many people mismanage time lie in their own attitudes, in a tendency to emphasize the wrong things: perfection, rather than excellence; activity, rather than action; efficiency, rather than effectiveness. Like the individual in the following case study, they also tend to find it hard to say 'no' and to delegate work to others.

---

### Case study: Mismanaging time.

Helen is the eldest of six children brought up in a remote rural community. Her upbringing was caring but strict and from an early age she was expected to help with her younger brothers and sisters. When her contemporaries were out enjoying themselves after school, she was usually busy with domestic chores.

During her early teens Helen decided that she would succeed at school in order to 'better herself' and get away from home. She did well in her A-levels, went on to study at a university some 200 miles away from her home and then obtained an accountancy qualification.

Now aged 33, Helen has had two jobs since qualifying, preferring to work as an accountant in a commercial organization to acting as an auditor. Though she has reached a fairly senior position in a medium-sized company, she feels dissatisfied and is uncertain about her next career move. Helen's problems stem from her view of herself as a 'servant', rather than a leader. Because she is not assertive with the company's senior managers — all of whom are male — they almost always succeed in pressing on her the urgency of their own particular needs. She feels it is less trouble to give in to these demands than to enter into debate about them. She cannot prioritize tasks and misses some important deadlines as a result.

Having always done everything for herself, Helen also finds it very difficult to delegate tasks to others, including her own secretary. As she regularly works a 12-hour day and takes work home at weekends, she is often tired and has little life outside the office.

Things came to a head when a new managing director joins the company. Keen on teamworking, he is impatient with Helen's explanation about not having had the time to complete an important set of accounts on schedule. Telling her to start taking control of her time and delegate more work to her staff, he warns her that he has no time for managers who behave like 'one-man bands'. Helen is obliged to start looking more carefully at how she uses her own and other people's time. The following activity helps her do so.

## Activity 6: How do you use your own time?

Analysing how you use your time can provide valuable insights into your effectiveness in any role. It can also help you focus on priorities, measure change and review progress.

Take a day in the near future when you know you will have a lot to do. Fill in the following time log with the activities you plan for the day and what you expect to achieve from each of them — their expected yield.

| Time log — planned | | |
| --- | --- | --- |
| Date | | |
| Time | Activities | Expected yield |
| 8.00 | | |
| 9.00 | | |
| 10.00 | | |
| 11.00 | | |
| 12.00 | | |
| 1.00 | | |
| 2.00 | | |
| 3.00 | | |
| 4.00 | | |
| 5.00 | | |
| 6.00 | | |
| 7.00 | | |

At the end of the day, complete the following time log and then consider how your planned use of time compares with how you actually used it, and whether you have achieved the yield you expected from each activity.

| Time log — actual | | |
|---|---|---|
| Date | | |
| Time | Activities | Yield |
| 8.00 | | |
| 9.00 | | |
| 10.00 | | |
| 11.00 | | |
| 12.00 | | |
| 1.00 | | |
| 2.00 | | |
| 3.00 | | |
| 4.00 | | |
| 5.00 | | |
| 6.00 | | |
| 7.00 | | |

Aim to complete the above activity for at least five different types of days, each of which includes a range of activities. After tackling this exercise, ask yourself the following questions:

■ How effective am I at planning my time?

■ Am I spending time on important activities or simply on urgent but unimportant ones?

■ How much time do I waste?

■ How much time do others 'rob' from me?

■ Do I spend enough time preparing for important tasks or encounters?

■ Do I spend enough time reviewing outcomes?

## Pointers for effective time management

We are all allotted the same 24 hours in each day. It is how we use this time that makes the difference,

Planning is the key to effective time management, and you should aim to plan around 75 per cent of your time. The following suggestions are intended to help you do this planning and so cut down on the amount of time you waste.

■ List your goals for the coming month.

■ List the activities that will enable you to reach these goals.

■ Identify activities that need to take priority if you are to achieve your goals.

■ Prune out trivial and unimportant tasks.

■ Identify activities which, though important, can usefully be delegated or deferred.

■ Allocate a time slot for each activity that reflects the priority you have given it. Use a time planner or diary for this purpose. And remember that time booked with yourself is just as important as a meeting or appointment with others.

■ If you are interrupted in the middle of an activity, take it up where you have left off as soon as possible. Do not let other people's priorities dictate your own.

■ Review your planned use of time against actual use of time at the end of each day.

## Learning to delegate

We have already touched on the importance of delegation in relation to time management. It is a skill which many executives lack at the start of their careers — and which some never acquire.

Learning how to delegate is really about developing faith in others and overcoming the feeling that you are the only person capable of getting things done. Whether you are responsible for a large team or a solitary individual, the following points should help you delegate successfully.

■ Aim to delegate whole jobs, rather than isolated tasks for which staff are unlikely to develop any sense of ownership.

■ Define the results you are looking for.

■ Discuss with your team the methods they can use to achieve these results.

■ Let them get on with the job by themselves but be there if they need your help. Interference defeats the whole object of delegation.

■ Hold regular and pre-arranged reviews of progress.

■ Give feedback when a job is completed.

## Activity 7: Producing a learning plan

Review this chapter and the activities you have already completed. Then divide a page into three sections under the following headings:

■ Observing and acquiring information

■ Processing and analysing information

■ Implementing decisions and taking action

Under each section note where you feel you need to learn more and where you need to improve your skills.

For each section produce one specific action to carry out during the coming week. When you have carried out that action, do the same with the other areas. It is only by being specific that you will make improvements. For example, if you have noted 'questioning and listening skills' as an area in which you need to improve, your aim for the next week could be: 'Before I make a statement or give an opinion, I will ask at least one open-ended question and then I will listen.'

If your targets are specific and measurable, you will find that this activity helps you achieve real improvements.

## Technical and professional skills and knowledge

We have made no attempt in this chapter to deal with skills and knowledge relevant to particular occupations and professions, but your effectiveness in the future will depend on ensuring that you continue to develop your skills in these areas.

This is obvious for those in the professions (such as medicine, law, accountancy and so on) but it is equally true for those who are in general management. Judicious reading is the best way of keeping up-to-date — and if you read nothing else, the *Harvard Business Review* and *Management Today* should keep you in touch!

# 7

# Meeting People on the Way

## Impressions and perceptions

You have now considered how you learn and what you have learnt in your life so far, and identified some of the key skills and competences still missing from your 'kitbag'. You have also thought about your personal and career goals and set in train plans that will lead you towards their fulfilment. All these processes are essential to the development of a successful career. On their own, however, they are not enough. To become an effective manager or professional, to influence people and, indeed, relate to them in all aspects of your life, you also need to develop a keen awareness of how your behaviour affects others.

All communication experts agree that the way people behave is at least as important as what they say and do. Tone of voice, facial expression, gesture, posture — even the clothes you wear — contribute to the impression you make on others. If that impression is a negative one, if you fail to inspire trust and confidence in people, they will not want you in their teams, as their boss or as their colleague.

There is little point in telling people they can trust you or feel comfortable working with you. Only the impression you create can trigger these emotions, and you can only learn to create a more favourable impression by observing closely the effect your behaviour has on others. This may seem obvious but all too often people are reluctant to change their behaviour — even when they pick up negative signals from those around them. The following examples, all based on real case histories, illustrate this point.

■ A management consultant had no trouble drumming up new business, but was finding it difficult to keep his clients. When a friend hinted that his abrupt manner and habit of interrupting others could be part of the trouble, he replied: 'I've always been like that and see no reason why I should change now'.

■ An experienced, well-qualified actuary had made dozens of job applications but none had so far led to a job offer. He tended to slouch back when he was sitting and to stretch out in what he thought was a friendly manner. A consultant who was coaching him in interview techniques suggested that this body language, which gave him a laid back and somewhat easy-going air, might have something to do with his failure to get beyond initial interview.

Rather than attempting to change his posture, this individual said he could not sit up straight because he was tall and lanky. Had he made some attempt to change his behaviour, he might have discovered that sitting up straight was not only comfortable, but could also help him make a positive impression on interviewers!

■ A bright young manager could not understand why she scored low in her appraisal when it came to receiving feedback from colleagues, bosses and subordinates. Told that people found her habit of speaking with arms firmly folded across her chest challenging and even intimidating, she said that in a man's world, woman had to be challenging. Again, this individual was making excuses for behaviour that others found off-putting, rather than trying to change her ways.

## Activity 1: Observing yourself

To begin seeing yourself as others see you, try recording one of your encounters with other people. It may be a conversation with friends, a meeting at work, an appraisal interview or any other kind of encounter. (You will, of course, need the consent of the other participants to record the meeting.) Then play back the recording and make notes assessing how the encounter has gone. Use the following questions to guide your thoughts.

■ Did you talk too much or too little?

■ Did you speak clearly and confidently? Did your voice sound too loud or too low?

■ Did you interrupt the other speakers? Did you sound interested in what they had to say? Did your comments seem to follow on from what others had said? Did you attempt to draw more reticent members of the group into the conversation?

Repeat this exercise every few weeks and keep the recordings you make, listening to them occasionally to check whether you are making progress.

## Managing encounters

Becoming aware of the impact of your behaviour on others is essential to the success of your relationships both at work and in other areas of your life. But if you are to manage your career successfully, it is equally important to take responsibility for all your encounters, be they job interviews, meetings with clients, appraisal interviews or team briefings.

By deciding in advance what you hope to achieve from an encounter, you can ensure that it becomes a two-way exchange and that you influence its outcome. When attending an appraisal interview, for instance, you may be tempted to wait for your boss to say what he or she thinks of your performance. But in fact, there is no reason why you should not go into the meeting with a clear idea of what you hope to achieve from it. Similarly you need not play a passive role at job interviews; if you plan in advance what you want to say, you will go a long way towards influencing the interviewer's perception of you as a candidate.

In any encounter the key to success lies in planning and in setting yourself clear objectives. So begin by asking yourself the following questions:

■    What do I hope to achieve from this meeting?

■    What are the other people hoping to achieve from the meeting?

If you are not clear as to why other people are attending a meeting, ask them or find out in some other way. Once you are clear about the objectives of a meeting, you can plan for it in the following ways.

■    Prepare your contributions. If you are not sure what is expected of you, find out.

■    Make sure you are aware of the role, status and relationships of the other participants.

■    If it is a formal meeting, make sure you understand the 'rules'.

Even at an impromptu encounter when there is no opportunity to plan in advance, you should take time to listen and consider your responses to others. A chance meeting in the lift can turn out to be as much of a milestone in your career as a formal interview!

During the meeting itself, you need to:

- Listen!

- Focus on what you know. It is a mistake to try to contribute to every item on the agenda. Sometimes asking just one or two pertinent questions can create a more positive impression than speaking at great length.

- Check that your contributions are relevant and understood.

- Ensure you understand what is happening and what is decided.

## Influencing and persuading

In many encounters your objective is likely to be to persuade others of your point of view. The influencing skills you demonstrate on these occasions will in turn probably influence other people's perceptions of you.

It is therefore important for your career development to plan for these encounters by:

- setting yourself clear objectives

- identifying as much common ground as possible between your position and that of others involved in the debate

- anticipating the range of possible alternatives to your point of view

- considering appropriate arguments to support your position — without, of course, becoming confrontational.

During the encounter itself, try to use questions to:

- clarify the agenda

- elicit information

■ establish rapport with the other parties

■ focus the discussion

■ move the discussion forward by building on ideas.

## Activity 2: Planning to persuade

Think of a situation in which you might want to bring someone around to your point of view. It could, for example, be a case of persuading the boss to give you a pay rise or of talking your bank manager into extending your overdraft facility.

Plan for this encounter by making a note of exactly what you hope to achieve from it. Then establish common ground by listing the ways in which your objective might benefit the other party as well as yourself. Finally, frame a series of questions calculated to help you manage the encounter.

## The art of self-promotion

Our culture tends to discourage people from talking about their achievements, often labelling such behaviour as conceited. This may be why individuals who devote considerable time and energy to promoting their organizations are often reluctant to promote themselves. Yet if you are to manage your career successfully, it is essential to master the art of self-promotion and let others understand what you have achieved.

You will not be accused of 'bragging' or being conceited as long as you stick to factual statements about what you have done and let others draw their own conclusions. There is no need to say, for example, that you have negotiated a 'great' contract for your company; stating the value of the contract will be much more effective.

You should also avoid making self-deprecating comments. For instance, rather than introducing yourself as 'only' a graduate trainee in the finance department, you could simply say you work in the finance department. Similarly, if you have a suggestion to make, it is not a good idea to say: 'You may think this is a stupid suggestion, but…'

## Activity 3: Blowing your own trumpet

Write a brief description of something you are proud to have done — not necessarily in connection with your work. Then spend no more than two minutes talking into a tape recorder about the same achievement. Play back the recording and consider whether you have managed to convey what you have done with enthusiasm — but without bragging. Finally, practise describing this achievement to a friend or colleague.

## Being seen and heard

Self-promotion is not only a question of telling people what you have achieved but also of being seen at conferences, seminars, meetings of professional bodies and similar events. So next time you are invited to one of these events, resist the temptation to spend yet another evening in front of the television and accept the invitation. You never know who you might meet or what you might learn.

If you are to promote yourself successfully you also need to develop the ability to make presentations. Begin with low-key events — perhaps talking to local sixth formers about your particular occupation — and gradually build up to more prestigious events. If you find public speaking difficult, see if you can give joint presentations with a more experienced speaker until you have built up your confidence. An advantage of sharing a platform with other speakers is that they can provide you with feedback about your performance.

You should also pay close attention to your audience, and as in any encounter with others, modify your behaviour in the light of their reaction. If, for instance, your audience tends to interrupt, consider the ground rules you laid down at the start of your talk, and next time make it clear that there will be plenty of time at the end for questions and comments.

## Activity 4: How effective is your self-marketing?

Answer the following questions to assess how well you are promoting yourself.

■ Are you proud of your accomplishments and do you find ways of letting people know what they are?

■ Do you seek feedback about your performance from colleagues, bosses, tutors and others?

■ Do you use this feedback to improve your performance?

■ Do you maintain contact with professionals in your field to make sure you know your value in the market-place and to help you determine future trends in the field?

■ Is your CV current, well-organized, concise and accurate?

■ Does your CV reflect the measurable achievements of your career?

## Networking

Developing and maintaining a network of contacts is critical at all stages of career development and not simply when a job change is on the cards. Networking is also good fun. Successful managers and professionals know this, tend to have a wide range of contacts and to use their networks proactively to promote themselves and their organizations. They realise that people they know are likely to be more helpful than strangers and that a network is a valuable source of information and advice.

Networks exist at all levels, in all environments, and are not exclusive to City heavyweights or those who have been to the 'right' school or university. If you count everyone you know, including those who have no connection with your work, you will be surprised at the extent of your own network. But like any other valuable asset, a network has to be nurtured and should not be viewed as a static resource. It is essential to maintain contact, especially with those you do not meet in the course of your daily round, and to keep your contacts informed of where you are and what you are doing. Remember also that networks are reciprocal, and respond when others contact you.

### Activity 5: Assessing the extent of your own network

Prepare a list of all the contacts who make up your own network. Include everyone you know — family, friends and neighbours, as well as those you know through your work. (Avoid being judgemental about their value. While some may not appear at first glance to be useful, they will all know people who are unknown to you.)

Make a note now to contact several people you have not been in touch with for some time. Behind all the value that a network may have for your career is the deeper value of having relationships and friendships with a range of people.

---

### Case study: A question of self-presentation

Diane was a product development manager in a software design company. Although she had extensive international experience and was recognized as an expert in her field, she was passed over for promotion to a general management role.

One of the company's directors took her to one side, explaining that she had failed to get the post because she appeared to lack the confidence and assertiveness needed in a senior management role. The fact that the company's chairman did not know who she was had not helped her prospects either.

This information helped Diane recognize that she needed to develop her communication skills if she wanted to grow and develop further. She also understood that she had failed to network adequately at senior levels in the organization. Though she felt a little uncomfortable about 'pushing herself forward', she came to accept that she could no longer afford to concentrate exclusively on her functional responsibilities but needed to invest time and effort in networking and making a stronger impression on others.

She decided to reorganize her time and delegate more work to her team to ensure that she had ample opportunities to meet senior people in the organization and become recognized as one of them. She also signed on for a management development programme, where she focused on upgrading her presentation skills. As a result of these efforts she began to be viewed far more positively, not only by colleagues but also by her team, who were pleased to be taking on more responsibility and developing their own skills.

---

Diane's story shows that 'books will be judged by their covers' — just as your presentation skills will be a powerful determinant of your success.

## Networks and job search

No introductory tool is as powerful as a reference from a personal contact. In fact, our own professional experience suggests that around 80 per cent of job offers come about as a direct or indirect result of such contacts. Some job seekers are diffident about networking in case they appear to be *asking* their contacts for a job. But effective networking is never that crude. It is not a case of asking people for a job but of informing them of your plans for the future, reminding them of your past achievements and asking for information or advice, which they are often only too happy to give.

How, then, can you use your network when looking for a new job or any other kind of new opportunity?

■ First, identify those individuals on your network list who may be in a position to give you relevant information or advice.

■ Then consider carefully whether to write or phone. A standard format letter, far from appearing mechanistic, sends a message of real purpose, and you can always add some personal comments to it. The letter should summarize in three paragraphs what you have achieved, what you are good at and what you are now looking for. The key message should be along the lines of: 'I hope I may come to you for advice when the occasion demands'. Alternatively you could ask for a meeting and say you will call to arrange it.

■ Think about sending a brief CV. This ensures that the facts about you are readily available and makes it easier for the recipient to talk about you to others.

■ While you are searching for a job, *all* your meetings — no matter what the occasion — should have these two items on the agenda: How can I add to people's knowledge about me? What can I achieve from this meeting that will lead to further action?

■ Be thoroughly prepared for meetings with contacts who are likely to be influential. You will probably not have another chance to talk to these individuals and if you have met them as a result of a third party introduction, good feedback on you will encourage the introducer to think of more contacts. Remember that network contacts will introduce you to others if they believe that this will in some way reflect well on themselves.

■ Keep those who have introduced you to others informed of your progress.

■ Check with anyone who gives you a lead whether they want it known that they have acted as a go-between. You should also think carefully before doing any name dropping: mentioning the wrong name to the wrong person can be very counter-productive.

Once you are settled in a new job, you should maintain your network in the following ways.

■ Inform and thank everyone you contacted originally, giving details of where you are and what you are doing.

■ Continue to keep in touch with key members of your network.

■ Recognize that you are part of other people's networks and respond in the way you now understand will be most appreciated.

## Women and networking

Many women find networking uncomfortable, and are worried that approaches to male contacts may be misconstrued. As a result, some have formed all-women networks. While these networks have often proved valuable, it would be unwise for any woman to exclude men entirely from her network. Men are, after all, still occupying the majority of the most senior and influential positions in organizations — and are likely to continue doing so unless women learn to develop and use their own networks to promote themselves!

### Case study: Networking for success

Sue graduated from Cambridge with a degree in history and then qualified as a solicitor. She spent the next 15 years in the civil service, where she became a specialist in European employment law.

By her late thirties, Sue was growing restless. She wanted a new challenge and felt drawn to the private sector, but was not sure where she should market her particular blend of knowledge, skills and experience. A chance encounter with an old friend from university days, however, suggested a possibility. On hearing that Sue was thinking of leaving the civil service, this friend, who was now working in an international law firm, suggested that she should write to Sir William, one of the firm's senior partners.

Sue followed this advice. In her letter to Sir William, she introduced herself and referred to their mutual acquaintance. She then explained that she was currently looking for a new position and briefly summarized the main achievements of her career to date. She concluded by saying: 'I hope I may come to you for advice when the occasion demands'.

A few days later she received a brief note acknowledging her letter. She heard nothing more until three months later, when she was surprised to receive a letter from the Brussels office of an international consulting organization. This organization had heard of Sue from Sir William and wanted to know if she was still available.

A series of interviews followed, which culminated in Sue receiving an offer of a job at almost twice her salary. She wrote to Sir William, thanking him for the introduction.

Soon Sue was commuting between London and Brussels and greatly enjoying the challenges of her new role. She knew that she had been recruited not only for her knowledge and experience of European employment law but also for her extensive network of contacts in Whitehall. So while getting to grips with her new job and with an organizational culture very different from the one she was used to, she also found time to maintain her old contacts. On one occasion she even flew to London specially to attend a former colleague's retirement party.

Having learnt from experience how useful networks could be, Sue would sometimes say to younger colleagues: 'You are only four contacts away from anyone in the world you want to meet!'

You may feel shy and ill at ease when you first start using your network of contacts. But as the character in the above case study discovered, networking is a key element in maintaining employability.

# 8

# Opening the Door to Interviews

## The essential tools

While Chapter 7 discussed the importance of self-marketing at all stages of your career, we now turn to how you can let prospective employers know of your achievements.

Before looking at how you can achieve success in job interviews, we will consider those two all-important self-marketing tools associated with the earlier stages of job search: the curriculum vitae (CV) and the approach letter.

The CV has one key function: to attract a potential employer's attention and hold it long enough to convince him or her to grant you an interview. It is possible to attract that attention by using unorthodox methods. A software design specialist, for instance, once sent a company his CV wrapped around half a model of a human brain; in the accompanying letter, this individual offered the company the other half of the brain if they gave him a job! Then there was the case of the international drinks company which advertised an opening in its marketing function and received hundreds of applications, including one that stood out from the rest because it arrived in an empty whisky bottle. These and similar gimmicks do sometimes work — but they can just as easily backfire if the recipient does not share the sender's sense of humour.

A less risky way of attracting the attention of potential employers is to adapt your CV to their particular requirements. If the job in which you are interested is in the voluntary sector, for example, you might highlight any charity work you have done in your spare time. Similarly, a CV sent to a travel company might stress those aspects of your career history or leisure interests which relate in some way to the travel business.

## The building blocks of your CV

As time passes, it becomes all too easy to forget much of what you have done and achieved. One way of making sure that you have all the information at your fingertips when you need it is to keep your CV up-to-date at all times, 'customizing' it as and when the need arises. Even when you are not looking to change jobs, you should find that the process of updating your CV will heighten your awareness of your own achievements and career objectives. This in turn will help you promote yourself at all stages of your career.

The two basic building blocks of any CV are a career outline and a list of achievements.

To draw up a career outline, prepare a detailed listing of bio-graphical data, including career history, education (starting with secondary schooling), training and interests. (You should find that looking back at the notes you made while working on Chapter 3 will help you in this task.) Set out this career history in reverse chrono-logical order, including the date on which you started and left each job or course.

The process of drawing up a list of achievements is one which we have already described in Chapter 4. Repeat it now by making a note of your successes to date in the form of vignettes (describing in each case the situation, action and yield). Then hone down the vignettes you consider most significant into 'bullet points' that can be incor-porated into your CV. This process will enable you to transform your CV from a traditional listing of positions you have held into a series of descriptions of the projects you have successfully undertaken. As well as being more appropriate in today's employment climate, updating your CV on a project basis will also enable you to identify future projects likely to further your progression in relation to an overall career plan.

Once you have outlined your career history and listed your achieve-ments, you need to turn your attention to the presentation of this information.

## Choosing the right format for your CV

The format you use will depend mainly on the type of career you have had to date and on the nature of the job you are seeking. The main options are listed below.

1.  The most common format sets out career history in reverse chronological order and for each job:

■ briefly states the organization's activity and size

■ provides job title and outline of responsibilities, and

■ lists key achievements in bullet points.

2. The functional CV lists jobs as above, but records achievements separately under headings covering the individual's areas of expertise, responsibility or function. For someone with a background in finance, for example, these headings might include audit, tax, management information and treasury. For a marketing professional, the headings might include sales promotion, market research and product development.

   The functional CV is most appropriate for a career made up of a series of jobs at similar levels of responsibility in several organizations. It can also be useful for individuals transferring to a totally new scene in which their previous skills and experience are transferable — for example, from military to civilian life.

3. The one-page summary, which may be appropriate for those seeking a very senior appointment or a portfolio of jobs, broadly follows the format of the first option above, but excludes achievements which are usually summarized in a covering letter. It is also useful for networking — a one-page summary being easier for the recipient to handle. Whichever format you use, your CV should also include the following items of information.

■ full name

■ address and telephone number

■ date of birth

■ education and qualifications in reverse chronological order

■ hobbies and interests if these are relevant to the position you are seeking, or if you have limited career experience.

You could give details of your marital status and nationality, though these items are not always considered essential.

## General tips for writing a CV

■ Write it with the needs of readers uppermost in your mind.

■ Use short, simple phrases rather than complete sentences.

■ Type it on good quality paper.

■ Keep to a *maximum* of two pages.

■ Do not make false or misleadingly ambiguous statements.

■ Make sure you account for every year of your life from the beginning of your secondary schooling.

Without departing from the above guidelines, try to produce a CV that is distinctive. You do not want this important document to seem 'branded' or look as though it had been written for you. Note people's reactions to your CV but remember that whatever they say, if your CV leads to an interview, it has fulfilled its main objective!

## Activity 1: A critical look at a CV

Study the following CV.

## Curriculum Vitae

| | |
|---|---|
| Name: | Paul M. Smith |
| Nationality: | Scottish |
| Status: | Married, one son |
| Education: | A-levels, Maths, Geography, Economics |
| | MA, Highlands University, economics |
| Interests: | Tennis, dog breeding, charity work, |
| | business. |
| Address: | 16 Orchard Lane, |
| | Newtown, |
| | Anyshire NW4 6JH |

## Career

| | |
|---|---|
| 1980-85 | Samson & Samson (ad. agency) |
| | Graduate trainee |
| | Associate director at age 26 |
| | Handled range of client accounts in retail, hospitality and food sectors. |
| | Helped company win account with major hotel group — hence promotion to associate director. |
| 1985-86 | Markowitz, Smith and Long (ad. agency) |
| | Founder partner — did not work out! |
| 1987-95 | Swells PLC (Chain of ladies' fashion stores) |
| | 1. Marketing manager |
| | Responsible for: liaison with advertising agencies, mail order marketing. |
| | Reduced advertising costs by 5 per cent. |
| | Restored profitability to mail order business. |
| | 2. Deputy marketing director |
| | Responsible for: shopfitting and design, creative services (graphics, etc.) customer service. Spearheaded company expansion into eastern Europe with opening of stores in Warsaw and Prague. Reorganised and retrained customer service staff. Creative services team won marketing industry award for creative excellence. |
| 1995 - | Redundant following acquisition of Swells by Dutch-owned conglomerate. They brought in their own senior management team. I could have stayed on but in a capacity which I felt was not commensurate with my experience and seniority. I am now doing some part-time consultancy work, mainly for clients in the retail sector. |

Now write a critique of the above CV, using the following questions to guide your thoughts.

- Has Paul Smith presented the information about his career in a way that highlights his achievements? How might the layout and presentation of the CV have been improved?
- Does Paul's CV include any information that he might have been wiser to leave out? Does his CV omit any information that should have been included?
- Does Paul account for every period of his working life?
- Would a potential employer reading this CV be able to invite Paul for an interview at short notice?
- If you were an employer looking for a marketing executive, would you invite Paul Smith for an interview?

When you have considered Paul Smith's original CV, compare it with the following version.

---

**Paul Smith**

British.      Date of birth: 12th May 1958      Married (one child).

**16, Orchard Lane, Newtown, Anyshire NW4 6JH**
**Tel: 01387-981350**

---

**CAREER**

1995-Date   **Independent Marketing Consultant**
            Clients include the Pets Emporium chain and other
            retailers

1987-1995   **Swells PLC** (Leading fashion retailer)

   '92-95   Deputy Marketing Director
            Responsible for shopfitting and design,
            creative services, customer service

   '87-'92  **Marketing Manager**
            Responsible for liaison with advertising agencies and
            mail order marketing

1986-1987 **Child Concern**
Voluntary worker
Responsible for marketing charity shops

1985-1986 **Markowitz, Smith and Long** (Advertising agency)
Founder Partner

1980-1985 **Samson & Samson** (Advertising Agency)

'84-'85 Associate Director
Responsible for oversight of client accounts in
hotel and catering and retail sectors

'81-'84 Account Manager
Responsible for hotel and catering client accounts

'80-'81 Graduate trainee

## CAREER HIGHLIGHTS

★ Spearheaded expansion of Swells PLC into Eastern Europe
with opening of stores in Warsaw and Prague.

★ Designed and launched in-house training programme
for customer service team at Swells. Subsequent survey
showed significantly increased levels of customer
satisfaction.

★ Creative services team for which I was responsible won
1993 Marketing Industry Award for graphics.

★ Negotiated 5 per cent reduction in Swells' advertising costs.

★ Restored profitability to Swells' mail order business with
launch of new 'next day' delivery service.

★ Won Longhouse Hotel Group contract for Sampson &
Sampson and promoted to post of associate director at
the age of 26.

## EDUCATION

1969-76 Newtown County Grammar School for Boys,
Newtown, Anyshire

1976-80 Highlands University —
MA in Economics

## *Activity 2: Writing your own CV*

When studying the two versions of Paul Smith's CV, you will probably have noticed that the second version is more succinct, that it highlights Paul's achievements much more clearly — and gives his phone number, which had been omitted originally! It also accounts for the mysterious gap in this individual's career following his brief period as founder partner of the advertising agency Markowitz, Smith and Long. The reasons why Paul did not remain with the agency and why he left Swells PLC have been left out of the CV but presented as positive career moves in the approach letter that appears later in this chapter.

Bearing in mind the points raised above, draw up your own CV. Adapt the document to the requirements of a job you have seen advertised, highlighting achievements that seem particularly relevant.

## The approach letter

An approach letter may be sent without a CV when the writer and recipient are both senior people or know each other well. It is also appropriate in situations where the 'comfort signals' are strong, and an accompanying CV might detract from them by introducing undue formality into the situation. If accompanying the CV, the letter should identify the achievements and features of your career history which are most relevant for the job you are seeking. Whether it is sent on its own or with a CV, the approach letter should aim to engage the reader's interest and present your credentials with a view to securing an interview. It should not simply duplicate the CV. The letter should take up no more than one page and include the following:

- your reason for writing

- a brief summary of your credentials and track record

- an explanation of what you believe you can offer the recipient.

Consider also whether to say that you will make contact with the recipient or await a response.

The following approach letter is one that our fictional jobseeker, Paul Smith, might have written to accompany his CV.

Your address

Contact name

Address

Date

Dear_____

I read with interest recent reports in the press announcing your company's plans to expand its European operations. As a marketing professional with a successful track record of managing similar expansions, I believe I could make a positive contribution to your organization at this critical time.

Throughout my career in advertising agencies and retail organizations I have sought opportunities for business expansion and product development. In my most recent position as deputy marketing director with the leading fashion retailer, Swells PLC, I initiated a move into the emerging eastern Europe market, where the company now has two highly successful stores.

When Swells was recently acquired by the Dutch-owned ABC group, I saw this as a suitable opportunity to seek new challenges. For the last few months I have worked as an independent marketing consultant, developing, among other assignments, a new marketing strategy for the Pets Emporium retail chain. In six weeks this strategy has increased the company's share of the petfood market by 3 per cent.

I am now looking for a general management role in an organization seeking to improve its market position, and would welcome the opportunity to meet you or one of your colleagues for a discussion. I enclose my CV and look forward to hearing from you.

Yours sincerely,

Paul Smith

## Activity 3: Writing an approach letter

Draft an approach letter to accompany the CV you drew up earlier on. Try to present your achievements in a way likely to engage the reader's interest and secure you an interview for a particular job you have seen advertised.

# 9

# Jumping the Interview Hurdle

## Approaching new 'clients'

Throughout this book we have encouraged you to view your career as a business: Me PLC. Like any business it needs a mission, clear objectives, attention to asset development, and good day-to-day management. It also needs a marketing strategy to ensure that colleagues, bosses and others are aware of the excellence of its 'product'.

As we have seen, this marketing strategy needs to inform all your dealings with others; it is, however, particularly important at job interviews, when you are attempting to 'sell' your product to a new client. This may seem an obvious point, yet all too often people arrive at interviews unprepared, with little knowledge of the company they hope to join and no idea of how they are going to convince the prospective employer of their suitability for the job. It is as if a company were to launch a new product without first researching the market or identifying what distinguishes the product from others on the market already!

In this chapter we will help you develop a more professional approach to selection interviews, while also looking at appraisal interviews, which can open the door to further success if you are already in an organization.

But first we invite you to consider a case study that touches on some of the issues we will be exploring in this chapter.

### Case study: A question of compromise

Hilary, a social science graduate from a modest background, envisaged a role for herself in a public or voluntary sector organization where she would be able to 'make a contribution to society'. Being bright and forward-looking, she took an MBA, recognizing that this might open doors which would otherwise be closed to her.

One of Hilary's weaknesses was her envy of some of the other graduates she knew, who, she felt, were offered good jobs because of their own or their parents' personal connections. She also resented having to network and make an effort to meet people who would support and assist her in achieving her career goals. Combined with her insistence on always dressing and behaving exactly as she pleased, these attitudes began to stand in the way of her ambitions.

Hilary's excellent academic qualifications gained her a number of interviews in public sector organizations and charities. But her uncompromising attitude meant that none of these interviews led to job offers. It took many disappointments before she came to recognize that she was wrecking her own chances of success. This recognition helped her modify the arrogant behaviour she had previously displayed at interviews — and when she applied for a challenging and sought-after position with an international aid agency, she was successful.

When you are preparing for interviews or other encounters, it is essential to evaluate the facts realistically, as Hilary did. You need to recognize if something is not working and modify your behaviour.

## Preparation: the key to success

In Chapter 7 we made the point that any encounter, however brief, needs attention and, where possible, planning in advance. This is perhaps more true of the job interview (both external and internal) than any other kind of encounter.

Begin your planning by finding out as much as you can about the organization you hope to join. If the organization is a public company, you should request a copy of its annual report from the company. You could also ask the company to send you some of its sales and promotional literature. Other possible sources of information include the business pages of the national newspapers, specialist journals covering the organization's business sector, libraries and information services and, where applicable, the headhunter or employment agency which arranged the interview.

Researching your prospective employer in these ways will help you respond confidently to questions about your possible role in the organization. The knowledge you display will also demonstrate your interest in the organization. But be careful about quoting your sources of information too extensively: it is wise to limit your comments to what you have learnt from the company's own published literature.

Having found out all you can about the organization, your next task is to discover what the interviewer is looking for. In trying to get inside this individual's mind, it is worth remembering that he or she is trying to find the best person for the job by ascertaining applicants' technical or functional skills, their ability to produce results and how well they are likely to fit in with the staff and the corporate environment.

You will probably be able to find information about the technical and functional skills the employer is looking for in the job description that many organizations send to applicants they invite for interview. Some organizations, particularly in the public sector, will also send a 'person specification' describing in more detail the qualities they are looking for in their ideal candidate. Such a document is clearly an invaluable aid to interview preparation, but even without it, you should be able to read between the lines of the job advertisement and job description to form a pretty clear idea of the kind of person being sought. Combine this creative interpretation of the documents at your disposal with your knowledge of the company, and you will come up with a list of skills, experiences and personal attributes not far removed from the company's own person specification.

Armed with this person specification, you will be in a position to establish how closely your own attributes match those the company is looking for. One way of doing this is to look back at the list of achievements you drew up in preparation for drafting your CV. Make a note of those which seem especially relevant to the job you hope to be offered, and then go through the same process with your technical skills and personal attributes — referring back if necessary to the notes you made while working through the activities in Chapter 4 of this book.

Thinking about your past successes and finding out how closely you match the company's ideal, will enable you to give coherent and confident answers to such questions as: 'What contribution would you be able to make to this organization?' or 'What do you view as your main achievements in your current position?' Systematic preparation will also help you anticipate many of the questions you are likely to be asked at the interview and to think about — and practise — how you might answer them.

## Activity 1: Questions and answers

Find a newspaper advertisement for a job which appears to match your aspirations and for which you might be a suitable candidate. Make sure the advertisement is one which gives a reasonably detailed description of the job and of the qualities sought in the successful candidate. Using this information, draw up a list of questions an interviewer would be likely to ask you if you had applied for the job. Try to think of questions that would elicit information about each of the following areas:

- Your current situation

- Career background

- Strengths and achievements

- Weaknesses

- Your perception of the job under discussion

- Reasons for applying

- Long-term career goals.

Now make notes as to how you might answer these questions — but without writing and memorizing a detailed 'script' which will make you sound over-prepared and lacking in spontaneity. Practise answering these questions, preferably working with another person who can assume the role of interviewer and give you feedback on your performance. Record your answers and play them back, using the following checklist to assess your performance.

- Were your answers clear and coherent?

- Were they concisely-worded and to the point?

- Did you answer in sufficient detail?

- Did you sound well-prepared?

- Did you sound confident?

- Did you give convincing reasons for applying for the job?

- Did you come across as genuinely enthusiastic about the job?

- Did you succeed in making a strong case for your suitability for the job?

If you are working with another person, ask him or her to comment on your manner and body language.

■   Did you look relaxed and confident?

■   Did you maintain appropriate eye-contact?

■   Did you smile enough?

■   Did your facial expression show interest and enthusiasm?

■   Did you appear to listen to the questions?

■   Did you talk too much or too little?

You will find that going through a similar process before a real job interview will help you recall your past achievements and give you the confidence which springs from knowing you are well prepared. It will also greatly reduce the likelihood of your being unable to answer any of the interviewer's questions.


## First impressions

You will never have a second chance to make a good first impression on a prospective employer, so your behaviour during those first few minutes of an interview is vitally important.

Below we list some of the things you can do in advance to make sure that the interview gets off to a good start.

1.   Get a good night's sleep in order to arrive at the interview feeling wide awake and alert. Arriving looking tired or, worse still, with a hangover, will definitely not help you make a good impression!

2.   Make sure that you know exactly where the interview is being held and how to get there. Allow plenty of time for the journey. A late arrival is likely to make you feel — and look — flustered, and could seriously damage your chance of success.

3.  Choose your clothes with care, aiming for an appearance that is both smart and appropriate for the environment in which you hope to work. But do not fall into the trap of buying something new especially for the interview: wear something you know will feel comfortable. Pay attention to all aspects of grooming and avoid using strong perfume or aftershave.

4.  Most people experience some nervousness or 'stage fright' before an important job interview, meeting or presentation. A surge of adrenalin will increase your alertness and is not necessarily a bad thing, but clearly you need to keep interview 'nerves' under control. You can do this by using a simple and inconspicuous relaxation technique while waiting to go into the interview room. Sit down and let your arms hang loosely by your side. Close your eyes and take several long, deep breaths. This will slow down your breathing rate and reduce other signs of nervousness, including trembling and sweaty palms. You will feel calmer and sound more confident if you follow this advice.

5.  While you are waiting, you could also try to visualise yourself replying to the interviewer's questions fluently and with conviction. This, too, will help you sound more confident.

6.  The interview effectively begins as soon as you enter the premises of your prospective employer, so be polite to the secretary or receptionist who shows you to the interview room and who may well be asked later on to comment on your behaviour.

7.  When you are shown into the interview room, greet the interviewer with a firm handshake, smile and look him or her in the eye.

8.  If you did not know in advance who your interviewer would be, make a mental note of his or her name in the first few minutes of the interview and use it as the conversation progresses.

9.  Finally, remember that a job interview will almost certainly leave you feeling tired and drained, so do not arrange more than one interview for the same day.

## The interview

During the interview itself your task is to convince the prospective employer that you are uniquely suited to the job under discussion. So refer mentally to the list of your achievements and use the interview as an opportunity to show Me PLC's 'product' in the best possible light. The following points are intended to help you do this.

1.   Listen carefully to the interviewer and pause (briefly) if you need to think about the purpose of a question or how you might best answer it.

2.   Smile when it is appropriate to do so and maintain eye-contact with the interviewer.

3.   Speak clearly and be sure to look and sound interested, positive and enthusiastic.

4.   Remember that the interviewer's objective is to find out as much about you as possible, so avoid giving one word answers. On the other hand, do not ramble on or go into unnecessary detail. When asked an open-ended question, about your present respon-sibilities, for instance, try to narrow the question down. You might say: 'My job covers three main areas: staff development, employee relations and remuneration. Which one would you like me to tell you about?' Having narrowed the focus of the question, you will then be able to give a short, succinct answer.

5.   *Never* run down your current or previous employer or colleagues. If you say that you do not get on with people in your current organization, people will be wary of asking you to join their team. So when you are asked why you left a previous job or why you want to leave a current job, stress positive reasons for seeking a change. Saying that you want to widen your experience, for instance, will create a far more favourable impression than saying that you cannot wait to leave because the company is in a mess and the boss a dictator!

7.   Rather than talking generally about how good you are at your job, describe and, where possible, quantify your achievements. ('Sales have increased by 20 per cent since I was appointed.') Use examples drawn from your experience to demonstrate your suit-ability for the job. If, for instance, the interviewer wants to know

how good you are at solving problems, you might say: 'Let me give you an example of how I tackled a problem just recently. The company gave me the task of deciding where to open three new sites. The problem was....'

8.   At all times accentuate your positive attributes. If you are asked how your team members are likely to describe you, for instance, you might say: 'She is supportive and listens to our ideas but she can be firm when it's needed!'

9.   Try to appear calm, but do not be lulled into copying the interviewer's body language, which in a job applicant may come across as too casual and relaxed.

10.  If you are asked to describe your weaknesses, explain what steps you are taking to turn them into strengths.

11.  Remember that an interview is a two-way exchange, rather like a game of tennis in which the ball is alternately in your half of the court and the interviewer's. Keeping this analogy in mind will help you manage the encounter and steer the conversation towards those aspects of your experience that you wish to stress and away from those you would prefer not to dwell on. Remember, too, that while the interviewer is trying to find out if you are the right person for the job, one of your objectives is to decide whether the organization and the job are right for you.

12.  Finally, do not consider the interview over until you have actually left the interview room — if not the building. After shaking your hand and saying goodbye, a skilled interviewer will often raise just one last point on the way to the door. This could be a decisive moment, so be prepared and do not let your guard down too soon.

Bearing the above points in mind, consider how effectively the job applicant in the following case study handles his interview.

## Case study: A marketing failure

**Interviewer:**     Ah, Mr Stephens, do come in. I'm Peter Wilkins. Very pleased to meet you. (They shake hands) Please sit down. Did you have any trouble finding us?

**Candidate:**     No.

**Interviewer:**     Good. Well, let's get down to business then. I see from your CV that you started your career as a civil engineer but that you've been working in marketing for several years now. That's quite an unusual switch, isn't?

**Candidate:**     Not really. You see, I was never that keen on engineering. It was just something I sort of drifted into — the way you do when you're young. I did maths and science A-levels and I was hoping to read Economics at university but my grades weren't good enough, so I got onto an engineering course through the clearance system. Then my first job was with a big civil engineering firm. I stayed there for about a year, which was a total disaster and I got out as soon as I could. Couldn't handle their macho culture. Then I did various odd jobs until I got a place on a marketing course. I really enjoyed that and then...

**Interviewer:**     Well, let's move on to your more recent experience. I see your last job was with the XYZ Food Group. Looking back at your two years in their marketing department, what do you see as your main achievements?

**Candidate:**     I believe I made a significant contribution to the firm's successful marketing strategy.

**Interviewer:**     Could you possibly be more specific?

**Candidate:**     Well, the company launched a campaign to increase its share of the baby food market, and I came up with some of the ideas for that campaign.

**Interviewer:**     Can you give me any examples of those ideas?

**Candidate:**     (Long pause) Not off the top of my head. I'm sure I'll think of some after this interview, though!

**Interviewer:** (Laughs politely) Yes, that's often the way. Now, can you tell me why you left XYZ?

**Candidate:** Well, quite frankly I didn't get on too well with my boss. (Scratches his chin, and looks at the carpet.)

**Interviewer:** So you left without having anything else lined up? That's a rather...er...brave thing to do in the current climate, isn't it?

**Candidate:** Well, not exactly. (Long pause) What actually happened was that the company was downsizing and I was made redundant.

**Interviewer:** And have you applied for many jobs since that happened?

**Candidate:** Dozens.

**Interviewer:** Why do you want to join this particular company?

**Candidate:** Well, the job sounds interesting.

**Interviewer:** Do you know very much about us?

**Candidate:** I've heard about you, of course.

**Interviewer:** Good things, I hope! Well, Mr Stephens, I think that's as far as we can take things at the moment — unless, of course, there is anything you would like to ask me?

**Candidate:** (mumbles) Not really.

**Interviewer:** (Rises and holds out his hand.) Thank you so much for coming. (They shake hands and walk together towards the door.) Do you have any more interviews lined up?

**Candidate:** I've got another one this afternoon and two more tomorrow.

**Interviewer:** Good luck with all of them!

## *Activity 2: An improved performance*

The applicant in the above case study has clearly failed to convince the interviewer that he is the best person for the job. His answers betray a lack of thought and preparation and are either too long and rambling or too short and uninformative. Without changing the biographical details, re-write these answers so that they present this applicant's record in a more favourable light. (You will need to exercise your imagination in giving examples of his achievements.)

## Evaluating the job offer

As we have already pointed out, a job interview is as much an occasion for you to assess a potential employer as for that employer to assess you. If the interview results in a job offer, you will have to think long and hard before accepting it. Taking a job that does not genuinely match your aspirations will soon leave you feeling demoralized and affect your performance. So look back at the notes you made while working through the activities in Chapters 2 and 3 and evaluate the job you have been offered against the factors that you know bring you satisfaction in your working life.

If the job does not appear to offer the challenges you are looking for, if the environment is not the kind in which you would enjoy working or if the location is inconvenient, write a letter politely rejecting the offer. But consider how you might maintain contact with those who interviewed you, and look upon the experience as a lesson in self-marketing, which will stand you in good stead throughout your career and not only in formal job interviews. Remember, life itself is an interview and even a chance encounter can open doors to new opportunities.

## Preparing for appraisal interviews

The majority of large organizations today use appraisal interviews to review employees' past performance and agree targets and objectives for the future. From a career management point of view appraisal interviews are also opportunities for you to make sure that your boss knows of your achievements and your contribution to the organization. In other words, they are important elements in your self-marketing strategy.

As with job interviews and other kinds of encounters, you need to learn to manage appraisal interviews if you are to influence their outcome. And once again, the secret of success lies in careful preparation.

You can prepare for an appraisal interview first by deciding what you hope to achieve from it. Then review your own performance, set your own objectives and decide what support you will need to attain those objectives. The following activity is designed to help you with this preparation.

## Activity 3: Reviewing past performance

List the responsibilities for your current (or most recent) job and consider the extent to which you have succeeded in carrying out each of these responsibilities. You may find it helpful to grade your performance on a scale of 1 - 5. Support your conclusions with examples of what you have achieved, be they improved sales figures, efficiency gains or other concrete achievements.

If you are working to targets and objectives agreed at a previous appraisal, consider the extent to which you have met these targets. Again, you could use a five-point scale, supported by examples, to measure your own progress.

Now list the skills and attributes which you are using in your job. Identify those areas in which you are confident of your own competence and those which might benefit from further development. Consider also whether your style of working with others is a help or a hindrance in the accomplishment of your goals. If it is a hindrance, make a note of what you might do to improve that style.

Finally, set your own targets for improving your performance and decide what support you would like from the organization to help you reach those targets.

## Managing appraisal interviews

The kind of preparation we have outlined above will enable you to play an active role in your appraisal interview and to use the occasion to further your own objectives. This does not mean, of course, that you should attempt to dominate the interview, but you should do all you can to ensure that the occasion is a genuine two-way exchange of views.

During the interview itself take care to listen carefully and ask questions to make sure you understand your manager's feedback. While taking care not to challenge the manager's right to make these criticisms, ask for examples that clarify how he or she sees your performance. If you disagree with these perceptions, state clearly — and without aggression — how you view your own performance and, again, support what you say with concrete examples of what you have done or achieved.

Aim to leave the interview with agreement about objectives, time scales and supporting actions. If there is to be a written record of the interview, make sure that you agree with what is recorded — and, if you do not, arrange for a further meeting to discuss it.

The following case study illustrates some of the points we have made about handling appraisal interviews.

## Case study: The negative halo effect

Hasan's relationship with his boss was far from satisfactory. He found it hard to put his finger on the cause of the trouble, though there had been one or two occasions when he knew his sales figures had been late or he had not provided sufficient information at meetings. But these occasions were few and far between. In most cases, he was well prepared for meetings and instrumental in ensuring that other members of the management group also had access to relevant information. The work of Hasan's team was generally acknowledged to be excellent, yet all his conversations with the boss were short and tetchy. It seemed impossible to prepare for one-to-one meetings because they invariably seemed to follow directions he had not expected.

Hasan thought the ratings he had been given at his last appraisal unfair but he accepted them. It seemed that he was suffering from a 'negative halo' effect so that a few small events were leading to a generally unsatisfactory perception of him. He decided that for his next annual appraisal he would prepare thoroughly by reviewing the year's work in detail.

When the boss, as expected, presented a prepared document with the poor ratings already 'in ink', Hasan said that he saw his own performance differently. He asked specific questions to establish the reasons for the boss's opinions. By sticking to the facts and asking for evidence, he was able to move the ratings to 'satisfactory'.

In discussing the future, he also managed to keep the discussion focused on specific steps and actions that needed to be taken. His thorough preparation and persistence in keeping to the point meant that the meeting did not finish within the scheduled time and a further meeting was arranged to confirm the agreed outcomes.

Hasan began to apply a more systematic approach to other meetings with his boss. Whereas previously he had waited passively for the boss to set up meetings, he now often took the initiative. He kept to the point, rarely attempted to deal with more than one or two key items at a time and whenever possible confirmed the outcomes of meetings in writing.

While he still wondered if he would ever feel comfortable with this boss, Hasan could now see the value of establishing a more business-like relationship with him. The work he had put into preparing for his appraisal had clearly begun to pay dividends.

Preparation, as Hasan discovered, is an essential ingredient of successful meetings. Try to think how you will manage your next meeting, what your objectives will be, and how the points you raise are likely to influence other people's perceptions of you.

# 10

# How not to Shoot
# Yourself in the Foot

## Politics is not a dirty word

People often blame their misfortunes or failures on office 'politics' while claiming that they themselves never play this dirty game. A more likely explanation is that these people have actually shot themselves in the foot because they have not played politics effectively enough.

Political skills are essential to organizational life and have always played a central part in shaping careers. We are not talking here about politics in the sense of manipulating or undermining others but about the ability to get on with people and, when necessary, win them over to your point of view. In this chapter we will focus on these political skills and consider how they can help you manage your career. But first, a word about organizations.

## The pervasiveness of politics

It is just about conceivable that in a very small organization or one dominated by a single personality there will be no office politics. But in the overwhelming majority of organizations there will be individuals and groups vying for power and scarce resources, protecting their turf and promoting their ideas or values. Since these are all political activities, organizations are, by definition, almost always political.

But the concept of politics is not a monolithic one, as there are always two sides to organizational life. There is the rational and objective side represented by formal meetings, manuals, job descriptions, rules and regulations and the like. Then there is everything else that goes on in organizations — the informal side of hurried discussions in corridors, unplanned meetings and other everyday encounters. This informal aspect of organizational life has no written rules or regulations and you cannot learn how it works by reading a manual. But it is the ability to negotiate a path through it that ultimately makes or breaks careers.

Political skills operate at two levels reflecting the two sides of organizational life. At one level are the influencing skills that you use when your aim is to motivate, control, direct or persuade people. All the ways in which you communicate what you want or find out what others want come under this heading. Then at the second level come the political skills used in pursuit of your 'personal agenda' — what you actually want out of your job or career or, indeed, out of life. The personal agenda is about building relationships, about spotting opportunities and about having a plan for Me PLC. If there are politics around, and there always are, then those who have no plans are usually the ones who lose out — who manage to shoot themselves in the foot.

Politics, then, can be seen as the interaction between personal and organizational agendas, or between different people's personal agendas.

As we have seen in Chapter 7, every day brings opportunities to present yourself to other people. How you do that creates impressions and opinions of you that are likely to carry considerable weight at turning points in your career. In spite of the growing use of assessment centres and other 'objective' methods of measuring potential, job selection is still a pretty subjective process where opinions, often based on just one or two episodes, can weigh against all the evidence that comes from psychological reports or detailed assessments. You may score high marks on these assessments but somehow that will not do you much good if the anecdotal evidence is against you. This may seem unfair and is probably what upsets so many people about politics. They see themselves playing a *good* game that is open and straight and trusting, while other people play a *bad* game that is concealed and devious and non-trusting. But that is only one way of interpreting what happens in organizations, and it does not always reflect the truth.

What psychologists call attribution theory suggests that we attribute our successes to our own brilliance or competence, and our failures to everybody else or to the world in general! In that sense it is more comforting to say: 'I lost out politically', than to say: 'I lost out because I was not actually the best person for the job'. The following diagram serves to illustrate this point.

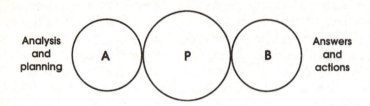

**Figure 10.1**   *Managing from A to B*

Side A is about planning, which many of us are good at because we have been trained to do it. Side B is about finding solutions, doing things and having answers. The middle bit is about people — and politics — and it is here that failure often occurs. This is because we may have done all the planning and analysis that a project requires, we know what should happen and we start making it happen but then run into problems because we have not obtained permission to go ahead — and not just from the boss. 'Permission' in this context means the support of other people in the organization who may not be directly involved in the project, but who will still have a view or who may be indirectly affected by your actions. This is one of the main ways in which people can sway themselves. They do not spend enough time thinking through such questions as:

■   Who do I need to talk to?

■   How should I present this?

■   Who else could conceivably be involved in what I am trying to do?

■   Will they support my proposals? If not, how can I get them 'on my side'?

These questions become increasingly important as careers progress. Although organizations are becoming flatter, it is still usually possible to talk about at least three levels of jobs.

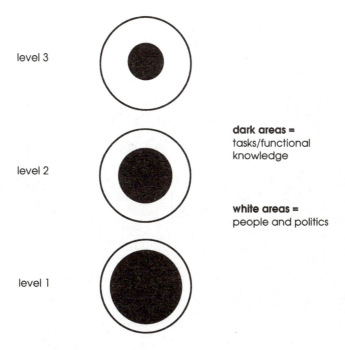

level 3

level 2

**dark areas =**
tasks/functional
knowledge

**white areas =**
people and politics

level 1

**Figure 10.2**    *From task to people*

At level 1, jobs are primarily about tasks, whether these be making or
selling things, processing information or delivering services directly
to customers. At level 2 where an accountant, say, leads a group of
accountants or a salesperson leads a sales team, the task element
generally becomes less important. People and politics are beginning
to assume greater importance at this level but the main managerial
tasks are to do with the group of people being supervised. At level 3,
directors or senior general managers still have to input a certain
amount of functional knowledge but this has now decreased considerably. While a directive style of management may work at level 2,
it is unlikely to do so at level 3, where a consultative style is more
appropriate.

It is how individuals perform in the 'white' areas in the above
diagram that decides whether they are successful or not. In the
authors' experience as executive coaches, people who fail at this level,
fail in the 'white' areas. This is often because they have reached senior
positions by virtue of their success in functional roles, but then find
that they lack the political skills needed to win people over and get

things done. Consequently, they may fail to form constructive relationships with colleagues, bosses or subordinates, and find that they
are always upsetting people. They may also fail to devote sufficient
time and energy to obtaining other people's permission for what they
want to do — which is what happened to the subject of our first case
study in this chapter.

---

### Case study: A clash of agendas

Kevin was a high-flier in his thirties, recently appointed to a
senior management position in a medium-sized manufacturing company in the north east of England. Though he
had been head-hunted for this post, he was viewed with some
suspicion both by colleagues and some of the company's
board members, one of whom described him as 'a plummy-
voiced southerner with more qualifications than sense'.

Four days after Christmas Kevin was asked to make a presentation about some organizational changes he was
proposing. Amid all the festivities of that time of year he had
little time to prepare himself or lobby the people who were
going to be at the meeting.

As soon as he began describing his still tentative restructuring
plans, the company's human resources director interrupted to
demand: 'Who are the people involved in all this? How many
job losses are you talking about?' Kevin should perhaps have
replied that he was only discussing the restructuring in general
terms and that it would not be appropriate to go into detail at
such an early stage. Nevertheless, he was thrown off balance
by the questions.

From then on the presentation went from bad to worse for
Kevin as one board member after another picked holes in his
arguments. Describing the meeting to his wife that evening he
said he could not understand why all these people had turned
against him. What he had not taken into account was other
people's agendas, especially their desire to impress the chief
executive by showing someone else up. He had also failed to
make sure before the meeting that he had enough people
behind his proposals. By not playing effective politics, in other
words, he had shot himself in the foot.

---

Once again, this case study illustrates the importance of preparation
in managing difficult situations. When preparing for a meeting, make
sure you think through what questions you may be asked and how
you might tactfully answer them.

## Activity 1

Have you ever found yourself isolated because you have tried to show other people how sharp and efficient you were? Have your efforts to give what you saw as constructive criticism ever backfired? Or have you perhaps sat in a meeting where you asked senior people one clever question too many? Write a description of an occasion when you fell into one of these or a similar trap.

## Improving your political skills

If the last activity has convinced you that your political skills are not all they should be, what can you do about it? The first stage is to identify the skills relevant to each stage of your professional development. Looking back to our three-level model on p.115, it is clear that at level 1 functional and technical skills predominate. Communication skills, including influencing, persuading, negotiating, questioning, listening and so on are also needed at this level but, together with leadership skills, they usually come to the fore only at level 2. All these people-type skills can be learnt and developed, and in earlier chapters of this book we have attempted to help you do so.

It is at level 3 that the more overtly political skills come into play. These may be more appropriately described as attributes or functions of disposition, rather than skills, since they include the following:

- quickness of thought

- energy, enthusiasm and stamina

- self-confidence

- creativity

- the ability to think laterally

- awareness and self-awareness

- flexibility.

The possession of these attributes can often be traced back to the way individuals were brought up, and how conflicts and personal relationships were dealt with in their family. But as we have seen in

Chapter 6, it is also quite possible to develop attributes such as awareness later in life. The same can be said of the personal management style that people need to succeed at the top of organizations — to succeed, in other words, politically.

## Personal management styles

Most managers have developed, consciously or otherwise, preferred ways of working and influencing others, which can be described as their management style. The effective manager, however, will be aware that there may be a need to modify his or her style in the light of changing circumstances.

For much of this century the prevailing view was that all effective managers shared certain common traits, including the ability to direct and take command of situations. In the 1960s and 1970s this was superseded by the idea that there was a range of styles from the authoritarian or directive to the democratic or participative, but that the latter were generally more effective.

In recent years a *situational* view of management and leadership style has evolved. This effectively says that there is no single style that can be described as 'the best', but that everything depends on the situation in which managers find themselves. There are, however, trends in organizations and society which mean that managers now need to be more flexible and less authoritarian than in the past. Rapid changes in technology, the globalization of business and the evolution of more fluid organizational structures favour leaders who can manage change and work collaboratively with colleagues — acting as coaches and facilitators, as opposed to commanders.

Consider the following 11 dimensions of managerial behaviour. Although we have presented them as polarities, developing an effective management style is not a question of choosing either one set of behaviours or another. Effectiveness will depend on the extent to which a manager can move between the poles in response to given situations. There will be some situations which call for individual initiative, and others which call for teamwork. An awareness of the need to modify style in the light of changing circumstances is a sign of political astuteness. Without this awareness it is all too easy to shoot yourself in the foot.

## *Dimensions of managerial behaviour*

Business

| | |
|---|---|
| entrepreneurial, individualist | team player |

Responsibility

| | |
|---|---|
| concerned with own needs and those of own unit/section | concerned with organization's needs and 'greater good' |

Vision

| | |
|---|---|
| pays close attention to detail (head down) | able to see the broad view, the big picture (head up) |

Corporate culture

| | |
|---|---|
| feels at home in one culture | able to adapt to a range of cultures |

Industry/political awareness

| | |
|---|---|
| knows own industry and environment and has little interest in the 'out there' | well-informed and interested in all major trends in politics, industry etc. |

Impact

| | |
|---|---|
| takes charge, directs, has command of situations. | supports, facilitates, coaches |

Thinking skills

| | |
|---|---|
| analytical, linear, able to diagnose and measure | creative, lateral, intuitive |

Change

| | |
|---|---|
| manages and maintains the status quo, reactive | takes initiatives, responds well to change, proactive |

Relationship style

| | |
|---|---|
| focuses on individuals' needs, one-to-one approach | attends to needs of groups, develops teams |

Communication style

| | |
|---|---|
| dogmatic, outspoken unambiguous | open, tolerates others' opinions, good listener |

Project management

| | |
|---|---|
| strength in own area of expertise | strength in breadth, teamwork |

## Activity 2: Assessing your own management style

Think of a situation in which you have had to assume a leadership or management role. Using the above list of managerial behaviours, write a short paragraph describing the management style you used in this situation. Then consider how appropriate and effective this style proved to be. If possible discuss your analysis with someone who is familiar with your management style.

### Case study: Old habits die hard

Stephen came from a large, working-class family and grew up in a northern industrial town. His father, a shipyard shop-steward, was a man of strong views who enjoyed banter round the table. The children were encouraged to express forthright views, and whoever lost an argument was often the butt of sarcasm. At an early age Stephen learnt the trick of demolishing other people's arguments or shouting them down before they did the same to him.

Stephen did well at school and was the first member of his family to go to university. He studied accountancy and moved rapidly through several companies to his current position as director of the transportation subsidiary of a major industrial group.

Soon after he joined the company, his management style began to cause friction with colleagues and subordinates. He liked argument, enjoyed showing how clever he was and was putting in very long hours in order not to 'miss anything'. The company, however, had recently brought in external consultants to help it develop teamworking and an open, participative management style — 'to show us all how to be nice to each other', as Stephen dismissively put it. But his sarcasm could not disguise the fact that his *macho* management style was at odds with the style the company was seeking to promote.

Eventually persuaded to look at his patterns of behaviour with the help of a coach, he began to see how he was repeating the behaviour that had allowed him to shine round the tea table of his boyhood. Slowly he came to accept that most issues could be dealt with in a much calmer and less confrontational way than he was used to employing. He realised he could still intervene forcibly when necessary but that he would lose nothing if he listened to people more carefully and encouraged them to open up. In many cases the answers to

problems would emerge without the need for him to do anything other than act as coach to those around him.
Stephen was still himself but with a much greater sense of
personal control. He could now observe himself in action
without becoming sucked into situations where he behaved
with hostility and aggression. Other people's opinions were no
longer the threat to his self-esteem that they had been.
The company's top management showed they recognised
these changes in Stephen's behaviour by promoting him
further. Only his father remained unimpressed, wanting to
know on Stephen's recent visits if the cat had got hold of his
tongue!

Like Stephen, you may need to take a close look at yourself to make
sure that patterns of behaviour which you found helpful when you
were a child are not now sabotaging your chances of success!

## Understanding the culture

In adopting a management style appropriate to a particular situation,
one of the factors you need to consider is the culture of the organization in which this situation has arisen. Organizational culture — or
ethos — can be defined as the shared beliefs, values, assumptions and
norms which influence the way people behave. It is 'the way we do
things here'.

Different cultures will call for different styles of management and
will also feel different politically. The stage an organization has
reached in its development is a factor in determining its culture, with
those which are in a start-up phase feeling very different from those
in a consolidation phase, in decay or going through rapid change.

When you join an organization — even as an external consultant
— it is like meeting a new tribe with all its rituals, codes and subtle
signals. In fact, it is probably worse because you may start out under
the impression that the members of the organization are speaking the
same language as you are, only to discover later how mistaken you
have been.

The entry phase into any organization is very important and very
difficult. The political *nous* you display in your first few days and weeks
will to a large extent determine your future success in that organization. There may be people who will try to test you out, put pressure

on you and shoot down any ideas you come up with on the grounds that these ideas 'are not invented here'. There may also be people who will see you as coming in and stepping on their turf and those who are resentful because they think they should have been appointed to your job. Until you know exactly what you are up against, it is probably best to observe, listen and act with caution, clarifying whenever possible what people expect of you.

Achieving this balance between caution and progress during the entry phase applies as much to independent consultants, temporary project managers and other 'peripheral' workers as to so-called permanent employees. If you are an independent, then the big trap that lies in wait for you is that people will confront you and say: 'Well, what would you do about this problem?' and you may be tempted to put your foot in it too soon. Far better to begin by listening and enabling people to feel more comfortable by sharing their thoughts and feelings about the situation with you. Only by enlisting the support and commitment of those involved will you succeed in implementing your ideas.

Below we list some of the issues you may need to think about when joining a new organization.

- The corporate culture and the forces that have shaped it, including any charismatic leaders, periods of rapid growth or decline and changes in ownership. A family firm that has recently been taken over by a larger company, for instance, may still retain some of the old ways of doing things, which newcomers ignore at their peril.

- The organization's dynamics and management style. If you are used to following orders, you may need to learn to take more initiative in an organization with a participative management style.

- The history of your own role. If it is a new one you will probably have more scope to develop it as you see fit than if you are following in somebody else's footsteps.

- The role, responsibilities and position of others in the organization — especially your key colleagues — and how these relate to your own new role.

## Case study: Culture change

At the age of 48 Patrick held a position one level below the board of a major construction company. His early career aspirations had been basically those of his father, who encouraged him to seek a naval career. Patrick was not averse to following in his father's footsteps, but failed an entrance board and entered merchant navy college instead. He did not complete his studies but took instead a qualification in civil engineering.

Patrick joined the company he was with until recently at the age of 22, and saw service all over the world at various remote locations. As an excellent and thoroughly reliable technician he gained rapid promotion, eventually becoming involved in major project development and negotiations with customers for multimillion pound projects.

In recent years many of the senior managers Patrick had known since his early twenties had reached retirement age. Their replacement by younger people from other industries brought about a change in the culture of the organization, and Patrick found it difficult to adapt to the new attitudes and values that now prevailed in the company he had known all his working life.

He was seen as one of the 'old guard' and did little to change that perception. In fact, he rather relished it as he felt that the company had always stood for reliability and solidity, whereas now it seemed to care only about quick and short-term profitability and — as he saw it — 'change for change's sake'.

This failure to adjust to the new culture meant that Patrick's management style was no longer in tune with that of his senior colleagues, and he was offered redundancy on favourable terms.

After a thorough review of his skills, interests and motivation, he then decided to take a master's degree in his field which would equip him to continue his career as a consultant to the industry that he had always known and in which he had an extensive range of contacts.

But the process of self-analysis and later of taking a degree had some unexpected results. Although Patrick had left his previous employer because of an inability to adapt to an alien culture, his growing self-awareness and ability to reflect on his past meant he was now better equipped to meet new challenges and adapt his management style to a variety of situations.

The ability to adapt to different cultures, highlighted by Patrick's experiences, is the key to managing change, especially if your career takes you into the world of consultancy where you will be working with a number of different clients.

## Managing relationships

Politics, as we have seen, is about the interaction between people and their different agendas. Who, then, are the people you need to consider and what are the relationships you need to manage if you are to play successful politics? The next activity is designed to help you answer this question.

### *Activity 4: mapping your relationships*

Make a list of every relationship in your working life that you can possibly think of. Begin with key relationships directly related to your current (or most recent) job. Then consider more remote relationships, including those with people in other parts of the organization.

Now consider your relationship with each of these people in turn, and write brief answers to the following questions:

■  What do these people want from me?

■  What do I want from them?

■  How do they tell me what they want?

■  How do I tell them what I want?

■  What are the main items/elements/products involved in my transactions with them?

■  How well is each relationship going?

■  Should I be investing more time and effort in it?

■  How do the key relationships in my working life link to each other?

Some of the more remote relationships you have identified may not seem very important now, but they could be influential in how you are perceived in the organization as a whole. It only takes one senior person to say they have never heard of you for your promotion prospects to disappear!

The following diagram may help remind you of the possible extent of your working relationships.

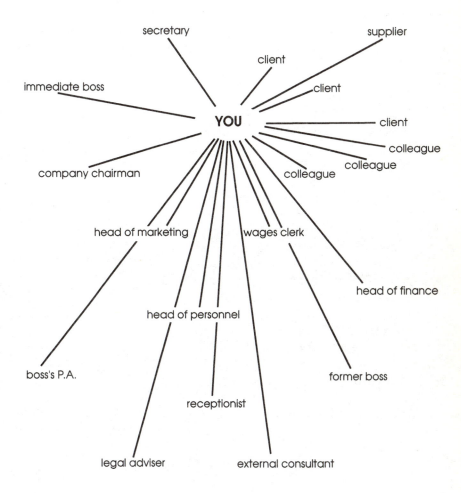

**Figure 10.3**   *Key relationships*

## Managing the relationship with your boss

If you are in employment, then probably your most important relationship is with your immediate boss. This relationship can be fraught with difficulty but it is up to you to manage it. You may well find that your boss is inaccessible, does not keep you informed of changes, rarely gives you feedback or even takes credit for your achievements. But before assuming that the boss is ill-intentioned or incompetent, ask yourself what pressures this individual may be under, and how your own behaviour may be discouraging him or her from communicating with you.

If you feel that there is room for improvement in your relationship with the boss, consider the following suggestions.

■ Ensure you keep your boss informed about what you are doing.

■ Show that you understand his or her concerns and needs. If you do not know what these are, then ask.

■ Seek support in advance of major tasks or changes.

■ Clarify what your boss expects from you.

■ Avoid causing irritation by missing deadlines, being late or not paying attention to the detail of your work.

■ Make efficient use of your time with the boss by:
    ■ having an agenda for your meetings;
    ■ taking notes to record meetings;
    ■ keeping focused;
    ■ having relevant data to hand.

■ Deliver what you say you are going to deliver.

■ Go to your boss with ideas, proposals and solutions as well as problems.

## Dealing with roadblocks

The above suggestions should help you deal with difficulties not only in your relationship with the boss, but also with other people. Inevitably, however, you will come across seemingly insurmountable difficulties in the course of your working life. What do you do, for example, if colleagues object to a proposal you have put forward or your boss decides, against your advice, to close a department down? You could, of course increase the vehemence of your arguments, but trying to push roadblocks over in this way is unlikely to do much good. Far better to remove the roadblocks gently by reversing and taking another route.

Often the most effective way of getting people to move from a seemingly fixed position is to put yourself in their shoes and show you understand their concerns. You may then find it possible to arrive at a win/win solution that meets everybody's concerns rather than a solution that represents one party's 'victory' over another.

## Activity 6: Developing empathy

Consider the following situation.

A well-established computing magazine is losing market share to its rivals. The magazine's ambitious young deputy editor proposes relaunching the publication as a downmarket tabloid newspaper and completely overhauling its contents. The marketing people are aghast. The magazine's production staff are up in arms. The editorial team is threatening to take industrial action if the relaunch goes ahead, while the editor refuses even to discuss the proposal. 'I'm not about to turn this magazine into a rag for computer games addicts!' he tells his deputy. The board of the large publishing group that owns the magazine greets the proposal with caution, but wants to hear more.

Put yourself in the shoes of each of these groups of players in turn. What arguments can you imagine the deputy editor putting forward in support of the proposed relaunch? Why do you think the others have reacted so negatively to the proposal? List the arguments that each group — including the board — is likely to put forward at a meeting to discuss the proposal. Then see if you can identify any common ground between them that could form the basis of a solution.

Now think of a situation involving a clash of interests that you have experienced at first hand. It may have occurred at work or in your personal life. Make a note of the arguments that you put forward — or wanted to put forward — in support of your own views, and then try to recall or imagine the opposing arguments. You should find that this process of empathizing with other people's points of view helps you find ways around difficulties that might previously have seemed insurmountable.

## Politics in the future

One question that may have occurred to you as you worked through this chapter is whether there will be more or less 'politics' as organizational structures become flatter and looser.

In the sense that a lot of politics in the past were about individuals trying to claw their way up stable hierarchical structures, the future may well be less political. However, in organizations made up of teams which are constantly formed and disbanded for specific projects, the ability to manage relationships, get on with people and win them over quickly will become more, not less, important. People with poor political skills will still end up shooting themselves in the foot and find that 'invitations' to join important projects or teams are not forthcoming.

# 11

# Getting fit for the Journey

## Managing emotions

We have now looked at many of the steps involved in managing a successful career. If you have carried out the activities suggested in earlier chapters, you should by this stage have a reasonably clear idea of where you have come from, where you want to go and how you intend to get there. In this chapter we will look at what you can do to make sure you are physically and mentally fit for this journey.

Our approach to the subject of mental fitness is based on the premise that your attitudes and emotions are within your own control, that you effectively *choose* the way you feel. Since experience suggests that the more positive we feel about tasks or activities the more likely we are to do them well, it follows that by managing your emotions you can go a long way towards achieving success.

Athletes have long understood this connection between attitudes and performance, often 'psyching' themselves up for sporting events by imagining themselves first past the winning post. We will now consider ways in which you too can develop a winner's frame of mind.

## Owning up to feelings and attitudes

The language we use to describe our feelings often betrays a reluctance to acknowledge that we actually own those feelings. We use such expressions as: 'You make me angry,' or 'This job is boring,' as if the emotions of anger or boredom somehow led an independent existence outside our minds. However, it is only by recognising the nature of our own feelings and attitudes and taking responsibility for them that we can begin to do something about them. That is what the character in the following case study discovered.

---

### Case study: A chip on the shoulder

Claudette, a Belgian-born biochemist married to an Englishman, had taught in a university in the Midlands for seven years. She was not happy in this setting and lost no opportunity to complain about the 'stuffy provincial' university and compare it unfavourably with the international drugs company where she had previously worked. She had few friends in her department.

Despite an impressive list of publications, promotion had so far eluded Claudette. She felt this was because of her gender and continental background, and did not acknowledge that her constant complaints about the university or her abrasive manner towards students and colleagues were in fact holding her back. She was therefore shocked when she accidentally overheard two students describing her in highly unflattering terms — particularly as both students were women.

After this incident Claudette thought long and hard about her position. She admitted to herself that her attitudes were largely responsible for her lack of career progression, but also came to the conclusion that she would find it difficult to change if she remained in an environment where her past behaviour had left her so isolated and unpopular. She decided to look for another job.

Claudette is now working in the research and development arm of a private sector company, where she feels more at home and where her new self-knowledge has enabled her to build positive relationships with colleagues and bosses. Her career is back on track.

---

After considering Claudette's history, take a look at yourself. Do you also have a 'chip on your shoulder' about something and is it standing in the way of your success?

## Activity 1: Keeping track of attitudes and emotions

In Chapter 6, we suggested that you should keep a journal in order to sharpen your powers of observation and become more aware of your surroundings. The same mechanism can also help raise your awareness of your own attitudes and feelings. So from now on, as well as recording the events of each day, make a note of your feelings about these events. You may find it helpful to arrange the entries in your journal under the following headings.

# Journal

**Date.....**

| Incidents/events | How I felt about what happened today | The lessons I learnt |
| --- | --- | --- |
| e.g. A client was rude to me. | I felt angry and upset. | Not to take these things so personally. |
| I was impatient with a Sales rep. | I felt I was in control of the situation. | Later I found out that our main competitor rates their products highly! So listen a bit more in the future. |

## Overcoming negative attitudes

Attitudes are habits of mind that we develop as we go through life: we are none of us born with a complete set of ready-made attitudes! Reflecting on your earlier life may have helped you identify the extent to which you have absorbed the attitudes of those around you — attitudes to success, to work, to education, to politics and so on.

People who tend to look for reasons why they cannot do what they would like to do, are often reflecting habits picked up in childhood. They may want to succeed, but if from an early age all their actions drew a negative response, they will find it difficult to take positive action in pursuit of their goals. They will, in other words, have developed the habit of procrastinating and making excuses for inaction.

You may never manage to overcome all your negative emotions and attitudes, but you can try working out why you feel the way you do — why certain events leave you shaking with anger or why you find it hard to believe you will ever fulfil your ambitions. Once you have discovered the underlying cause of these negative attitudes you will be in a better position to replace them with more positive ways of looking at things.

## Activity 2: Reviewing old habits and developing new ones

Make a list of some of your positive attitudes. Are you, for example, optimistic, generous, patient, good-humoured or confident? Now list your negative attitudes. Are you, for example, prone to feelings of inadequacy, anxiety, anger, guilt, frustration or loneliness? When you have completed your list, look back at the autobiographical notes you made while working through Chapter 3 and consider whether some of these bad habits of mind are playbacks of old scenarios that are no longer relevant. Write a brief paragraph analysing the probable causes of the negative attitudes you have identified in yourself.

Finally make a list of the positive attitudes that you currently lack but would like to develop.

### Case study: Alternatives to despair

After excelling at school and gaining a first class honours degree, Chris went on to take a PhD which he confidently expected would lead to an academic career. But although his thesis was well-received, there were few openings in the obscure academic discipline in which Chris had specialized and he did not find a position as a don, perhaps because he was not sufficiently persistent in his search.

By the time Chris had completed his PhD, his wife, whom he had met while they were both undergraduates, was embarked on a career in health service management. Not knowing what else do to, Chris drifted into an administrative job in the health service.

From the start he knew he was not suited to this type of work but his intelligence meant that he was soon promoted to a junior management position. As he slowly climbed up the health service bureaucracy, his dissatisfaction made him increasingly cynical. Asked why he stayed in a job he so obviously loathed, he would say it was an easy way of earning a living — and anyway, what else could he possibly do? When friends suggested other careers, he always came up with half a dozen reasons for not pursuing these alternatives.

Instead of exploring possibilities, Chris allowed the years to go by and threw himself into a variety of leisure activities, becoming in the process something of a connoisseur of antique furniture. But by his late thirties these interests were not sufficient to compensate for the misery of his working hours. The strain began to tell on his marriage, but he found it difficult to discuss his problems with his wife who was wrapped up in her own successful career.

Then Chris began an affair with a woman 15 years his junior and abruptly left his wife in the belief that this new relationship would help him shake off his depression. It did not happen. He still felt like a prisoner in his job, and his new domestic arrangements brought their own pressures and strains, which in time led to a complete physical and mental breakdown.

It was while Chris was recovering from this breakdown that a psychologist helped him appreciate that his attitudes and emotions were within his own control, that if life had become a prison, it was one of his own making. As he began analysing these attitudes and emotions, he realised that he had never really recovered from the early disappointment of his hopes of an academic career. This one set-back had convinced him he would never be able to do what he really wanted.

After identifying the origin of his negative attitudes, Chris began to see that there might in fact be alternatives to the life he had been pursuing. He reviewed his skills, interests and motivation and came to the conclusion that his knowledge of antiques might be put to good use.

Chris is now working as a valuer in a leading auction house and hopes in time to start up his own antiques business. He has finally discovered that life is full of possibilities for those willing to look for them. Although his wife has so far refused to take him back, with his new 'can do' attitude Chris is confident that he will eventually persuade her to do so.

Do you have a 'can do' attitude or do you look for reasons not to do things? As Chris discovered, it is important to identify the origins of negative attitudes — and to watch out for signs of stress before they get out of hand.

## Cultivating new attitudes

It takes a long time to unlearn the bad habits of a lifetime and develop new, more positive ways of thinking. The first step in this process, as we have seen, is to gain an understanding of how you developed your existing attitudes.

The next step is to stop blaming external circumstances, bad luck or other people when something goes wrong. Instead, ask yourself what *you* can do about the situation. In this connection it may be sensible to stay away from the 'moaners' who can be found in every group of people. These individuals tend to ignore what they can do about the problems they have identified, and their negative attitudes can easily rub off on you. So the next time someone tries to engage you in a conversation of the 'ain't it awful' variety, walk away or point out that the boss, the organization, the traffic or even the weather are not, in fact, that bad and may even have their positive aspects!

The process of developing positive attitudes also involves learning to listen to yourself. The next time you feel yourself becoming angry, impatient or frustrated, try following this simple procedure. Find a quiet room or corner, and shut the door or turn your back on whoever else is in the room. Sit down and breathe deeply for several minutes. Then ask yourself: 'Why am I feeling this way?' You are likely to find that as you sit quietly looking for a rational explanation, the negative emotion begins to subside, leaving you better able to deal with the situation that triggered it off.

### Activity 3: Listing the good things

Another strategy for managing negative feelings is to make a list of those areas of your life that you feel most positive about, be they relationships, activities that bring you satisfaction, or events and places that you associate with pleasurable experiences. Draw up this list and try to memorize it so that you have a ready set of vivid images that you can recall instantly. Then when those negative emotions begin to well up, focus on some of the items on your list of 'good things'.

### Finding yourself a mentor

In examining existing attitudes and cultivating new ones, the help of a mentor is often invaluable. The traditional view of mentoring was of senior managers showing newcomers the ropes — and in the process extending their own influence within the organization. Today, the concept has wider application and is perhaps more accurately described as 'coaching'. Although many formal mentoring schemes are designed to help integrate graduate recruits into organizations, there is growing recognition that the one-to-one support offered by a mentoring or coaching relationship can benefit individuals at all stages of their professional development, not just at the entry level.

If you do not work for an organization that provides this form of support, you may want to find your own coach or mentor. Any individual can take on this role provided he or she enjoys your trust and respect and is willing to act as a confidential sounding board, critic and source of advice. It is possible that your boss or a more experienced colleague could fill this role in your life. However, someone from outside your organization is more likely to be able to provide the confidential 'safe house' environment that is crucial to the success of the coaching process. This is one reason why a growing number of people today are turning to professional coaching as an alternative both to informal mentoring relationships and to traditional training courses, which are generally more effective in developing technical or functional skills than tackling 'soft' areas such as attitudes and values.

An effective relationship with a coach or mentor can help you develop self-awareness, gain an insight into your attitudes and cultivate the positive attitudes and assertive forms of behaviour associated with success. An example of how coaching can set this process in train is provided by the following case study.

## Case study: Outgrowing old habits

Harriet, who headed the accounts department of a transportation company, was coming under increasing pressure from her boss, the company's managing director. A man known for his poor communication skills, he refused to hold regular team meetings and tended instead to deal with people and problems on an ad hoc basis.

Harriet's meetings with the MD were always unstructured, covering topics she had not expected, and often ending in stormy rows. She would become especially annoyed when he involved others in work or decisions that properly fell within her domain. The MD, for his part, would criticise Harriet for failing to push through work changes involving colleagues over whom she had no direct authority. Harriet, who prided herself on being well-organized and preferred to work within clearly defined boundaries, found this way of operating extremely difficult to handle and made no effort to disguise her feelings. Eventually a senior colleague, appreciating the severe stress Harriet was under, persuaded her to sign up for a one-to-one management development programme. With the encouragement of her coach on this programme, she started keeping a journal in which she focused on meetings or encounters that had been unsatisfactory, as well as recording those where all went well. This process helped her see how badly she had always handled interactions with the boss, either escaping into a sulky silence or else growing so angry that rational discussion became impossible.

Having identified some of her own problems, she began to take the initiative in her relations with the MD (much against her inclination) and booked meetings with him to focus on one major issue at a time. She also wrote to colleagues when changes in working arrangements were due to take place and sent copies to the boss, whereas previously she had often relied on oral agreements.

One immediate effect of these measures was a reduction in the number of ad hoc interactions where she could be 'wrong footed' by appearing unprepared.

While the situation may never be perfect, Harriet is now feeling much more positive about her work. Colleagues seem to treat her with greater respect, actually seeking out her advice before acting. As a result of her growing confidence she is able to deal assertively with situations which in the past would have overwhelmed her. When the boss introduces a subject she is not prepared for, she listens for a few minutes, rises to her feet and says she will need a day or two to look into the matter. Then she leaves the room!

## Keeping away from stress

If you are to become fit in mind and body for the journey through life, you must learn how to cope with stress.

Stress is no more than a natural reaction to threats and challenges.When, for example, you are driving a car and suddenly notice another vehicle apparently careering towards you, your heart rate increases, your muscles tense and your mind becomes unusually alert. These are the physical symptoms that prepared our primitive ancestors for 'fight or flight' in the face of physical danger, and they still enable us to deal with potentially life-threatening situations. The energy released by the stress reaction also helps us cope with situations that may not pose a physical threat but are nevertheless challenging: examinations, job interviews or public speaking engagements come to mind as occasions when a certain amount of stress can enhance performance.

Often, however, there is no immediate outlet for the physical and mental energy released by stress. Far from finding expression in 'fight or flight', the stress triggered by disagreements with others, cancelled trains or missed opportunities is more likely to leave you feeling angry, powerless and frustrated. If these stress reactions become frequent and intense they can end up damaging both your physical and mental health.

In order to deal with stress, you need to be able to recognize its symptoms. The next activity is designed to help you do that.

## Activity 3: Diagnosing the symptoms of stress

We have divided some of the more common symptoms of stress into two categories: those that reflect *anxiety* that something unpleasant is about to happen, and those that tend to follow disappointment and lead to *depression*. Look at the following list of symptoms and make a note of any that you recognize in yourself. If you occasionally display one or two signs of stress, there is probably no need to worry, but if the symptoms persist or multiply, you may need to do something about them.

### Stress symptoms

| Anxiety | Depression |
| --- | --- |
| agitation | listlessness and boredom |
| insomnia | tiredness |
| increased food consumption | loss of appetite |
| excessive drinking, smoking | memory loss |
| rapid heartbeat, high blood pressure | sense of worthlessness |
| troubled breathing | feelings of rejection |
| heavy perspiration | lack of interest in sex |
| poor concentration | pessimism and despondency |
| indecisiveness | social withdrawal |
| aggression | suspicion |
| compulsive talking | moaning |
| over-attention to detail | low productivity |

The above list is not, of course, exhaustive and there may be other symptoms that you have experienced which you could add to your own list.

There is a common misconception that hard work and long hours cause stress. But, in fact, if you think of business leaders, politicians or others in position of power, they often seem to thrive on heavy workloads. This is because it is not hard work and long hours in themselves that cause stress but the conflict that often arises between the demands of our work and our own needs and desires. If you have few interests outside your work you may be quite happy to put in a 12 hour day at the office. On the other hand, if you want to pursue your own interests, lead an active social life or spend time with your children, then such long hours can be extremely stressful.

We allow ourselves to become stressed when we repeatedly respond to the demands of others, rather than our own needs and desires. This habit may stem from a belief that admitting to difficulties is a sign of weakness or perhaps that no one else can be trusted to do things as efficiently as we can. Tension between conflicting values can also lead to stress — for example, if you find yourself having to lie or cover up for your boss against your own inclinations. Dealing with the conflicting demands that cause stress, therefore, involves learning to be assertive about our own needs, priorities and values.

There is also a link between the kind of negative thinking we looked at earlier in this chapter and the extent to which particular situations cause us stress. Sitting in a traffic jam can be stressful, but only if you allow it to be. If you choose to see that half hour's delay on the motorway as an unexpected gift of time, you can enjoy listening to a tape, a programme on your car radio, or perhaps simply the opportunity to be alone with your thoughts and day-dreams. You might even use the space provided by the delay to practise relaxation techniques.

Whatever the causes of stress in your own life, learning how to relax will mitigate their effects. There are many books, audio and video tapes available today which teach relaxation techniques. Some techniques rely heavily on physical exercises, while others are more visual in their approach. You need to find out which technique works for you and then get into the habit of using it regularly.

## Activity 4: Dealing with stress

Think of a situation which you have recently experienced and found stressful. (You may find that looking back through your journal will help jog your memory for this activity.) Write a few paragraphs analysing the causes of your stress reaction and how you might have dealt with the situation to make it less stressful. The following questions will help guide your thoughts.

■ Was there a conflict between what you wanted to do in this situation and what other people expected of you?

■ Could this conflict have been resolved — through better time management or more assertive behaviour, for example?

■ Did you choose to see the situation as stressful?

■ How else could you have viewed and handled the situation?

## Physical fitness

There is a close connection between physical and mental health, and if you are going to run the race of life you need to pay close attention to both. Good health will help you rise to the challenges you will meet on the way and increase your resistance to stress. If you feel and look run down and stressed, on the other hand, other people's perceptions of you will be less positive than they might be and you could easily miss important opportunities.

Detailed advice on physical fitness is beyond the scope of this book, the basics, however, are clear.

■ Watch your weight by keeping to a balanced diet low in fats and sugar and high in fibre.

■ If you smoke, give up the habit. Smoking is not only bad for your health but increasingly unacceptable in social situations.

■ Cut down your consumption of alcohol and other recreational drugs.

■ Take regular exercise. Find a physical activity you actually enjoy: otherwise you will soon be making excuses for not taking exercise.

We have now looked at the importance of developing positive attitudes, managing stress and maintaining a healthy body. These various aspects of fitness are inter-related since negative thinking is likely to lead to stress and a whole host of stress-related physical ailments. Our final case study in this chapter attempts to show how tackling negative attitudes can help resolve other problems.

### Case study: A stalled career

Andrew was a civil engineering graduate with a post-graduate qualification in accountancy. For the past five years he had been working as a projects manager in a construction company, where his role was to provide the managing director with technical and financial support. His previous post as assistant to the company's technical director had carried similar responsibilities.

Now aged 33, Andrew felt he was not making any progress in his career and this led him to seek professional help from an executive coaching consultancy that he had heard of from a colleague.

It was immediately obvious to the consultant assigned to this case that Andrew's problems were not confined to his stalled career. His attitude to the world was cynical and rather grudging. Physically, he was somewhat unattractive, being around 20 pounds overweight. In a misguided effort to compensate for this disadvantage, he had adopted a flamboyant style of dress clearly out of place in the conventional environment in which he worked. His marriage, too, was going through a difficult patch, not helped by financial pressures brought about by a large mortgage and an assortment of credit card debts.

Throughout his career so far Andrew had been a 'number 2' man, accustomed to putting together facts and relying on his 'number 1' to make the decisions. The only place where he was able to adopt a more dominant attitude was at home, where he tended to talk down to his wife, a veterinary nurse who already felt inferior to him because she did not have a degree.

The consultant's first task was to help Andrew see himself as a potential manager, rather than an eternal assistant. To this end he advised Andrew to start dieting and to adopt a more sober sartorial style. After taking steps, his appearance began to improve.

Tackling his cynicism took longer. This attitude showed itself in his lack of respect for the senior managers in his company whom he regarded as his intellectual inferiors. Though he thought like a 'number 2', he felt he should be at least a general manager. The coaching sessions with his consultant focused on helping him think of himself as a manager working with other people and not just a well-qualified individual to whom the world owed a living.

Some months after the coaching sessions began, Andrew's MD told him he was to be made redundant unless another job within the company could be found for him. He was interviewed by one of the firm's senior managers for a position as her assistant but although he thought the interview had gone well, he was not offered the job.

After discussions with his coach he decided that a period in consultancy would enhance his stature in the job market, and he began to apply to consultancy firms. Although his qualifications and to some extent his work record secured him a good selection of interviews, his arrogant and unpolished attitude ensured that these did not lead to job offers. However, further work with his coach, including interview role-plays recorded on video, helped him see himself as others saw him and persuaded him to change his approach somewhat. In due course he received an offer from a small consultancy firm. He started work as a consultant but after a few months it became obvious that he was going to fail in this new role. He objected to working long hours without being paid overtime and found it difficult to reach decisions, though he could comfortably assemble the appropriate facts.

At the end of the year Andrew was given his notice. But by then he had acquired some consultancy skills and become more accustomed to the pattern of work and to taking decisions. Having now worked with a wider variety of people than he had come across in his previous company, he was also less inclined to view himself as intellectually superior to everyone else. After further work on his attitudes with his coach, he relaunched himself on the unsuspecting world of consultancy.

Within a few weeks he was offered a management post in a major consultancy firm. Away from people who had known him as 'the MD's fat assistant with the loud ties' or as a failed consultant, Andrew began to blossom. With the conflict between his aspirations and actual position resolved, his relationship with his wife also began to improve.

As Andrew's experience suggests, our 'fate' is always bound up with our attitudes — and attitudes can always be changed.

# 12

# Is your Parachute in Place?

## Review of goals

You have probably now filled several notebooks with your daily journal entries and all the other types of writing we have asked you to do as you worked your way through the activities in this book. In the process you will have increased your understanding of the factors that have influenced your life and career so far, the skills you have acquired and those you still need to acquire or develop further. You will have started taking greater responsibility for your own career development and personal growth since you know that no one else will do this for you. You will also have identified new goals and embarked on the journey towards their achievement. Your parachute should now be in place as you prepare to take off towards the future you want for yourself.

At this point it may be useful to pause and look back at all the writing you have done, particularly at the goals you set yourself while working through Chapter 5. It may be many weeks or even months since you did this work and much may have changed during that time. Now is the time to consider whether those goals still describe who you want to be and what you want to do, and, if necessary, to establish new goals. The first activity in this chapter is intended to help you in that task.

## Activity 1: Writing your own Who's Who entry.

Ten years from now, what would you like *Who's Who* to say about you? What achievements would you like to see listed there? Cast your mind into the future and write your own *Who's Who* entry.

Then consider what skills and experiences you still need to develop and what else you need to do if you are to turn the future described in that entry into reality. Compare your notes with those you made while working through Chapter 5 and ask yourself whether the goals you identified at that point — and the plans you made to enable you to achieve them — are still valid.

## Coping with the unexpected

Do not worry if the activity you have just carried out has caused you to adjust your plans; that does not detract from the value of the original planning process. Goals and plans are not hewn in marble. The unexpected is always lurking around the next corner to derail them, but if you did not have a plan in the first place you would not know where you were going or if you had been derailed!

If you have your parachute in place — if you are constantly learning and have cultivated your network — then even if something goes wrong, you will be able to cope. You have to look at the unexpected in relation to your overall goals and ask yourself what impact it will have on those goals. One disappointment need not be the end of the world, and an apparent setback, a sudden change of circumstances can even open doors to new opportunities.

### Case study: An unexpected opportunity

David had joined a major British textile manufacturer shortly after leaving university with a degree in textile engineering. He made steady progress in the company's research and development function before switching to general management in his late twenties. By the age of 36 he was managing one of the company's plants in Wales, a position which he saw as a stepping stone to a senior role in the company's head office. His ultimate goal was to join the company's board.

The company then became the unexpected target of a takeover by one of its international competitors. But having restored the Welsh plant to profitability and cut its costs by instigating a major programme to multiskill the workforce, David was not too worried about his own position. His new employers had in any case given assurances that they would leave the existing management structure intact for the time being.

David was right in supposing that his new bosses would appreciate his value to the organization. What he did not foresee was that they would have their own ideas about his future. Instead of offering David the job he had been expecting, they asked him to take over the running of one of their plants in California. This was a challenging position, offering a generous remuneration package — but it was not what David had planned for the next stage of his career. He hesitated, but only briefly, before accepting the offer.

A bachelor, David did not find it difficult to settle down in an unfamiliar environment and soon rose to the challenges of his new position. His goal was still a board level job back in the UK, but he was now aware of other possibilities, including a top job in the parent company. The unexpected had turned out to open doors to new opportunities, though David realized that without his earlier planning and the strong sense of direction this had given him, he would probably not have been offered the job in the USA.

After considering this case study, you might find it useful to think about occasions when your own plans did not turn out quite as you had expected. Were you able to turn the unexpected into an opportunity?

## Skills for life and employability

We have already suggested that you carry out an audit of your knowledge, skills and experience. Now is the time to look again at the contents of your 'kitbag' and ensure that you are properly equipped for the journey ahead. Among the life skills and attributes particularly important in relation to developing your employability, the following loom large.

- self-awareness
- the ability to learn
- an open mind
- good time management
- the ability to balance the demands of your work with those of other aspects of your life
- the ability to manage stress
- self-marketing
- networking
- problem-solving
- adaptability to change
- political awareness
- empathy
- physical and emotional fitness
- the ability to manage your financial affairs.

## Activity 1: Re-examining the contents of your kitbag

Write a brief account of what you have done since starting work on this book to develop each of the life skills and attributes listed above. This activity is intended to help you identify any areas you may have neglected, and should enable you to make up for lost time. If your finances are still in a mess, for example, see if a repetition of the financial audit you carried out earlier on enables you to improve your financial management. Similarly, if you still have trouble managing your time, you may find that another analysis of how you spend your days helps you find time you never knew you had.

Make a list of the skills that are especially important to you in your chosen field of endeavour. Keep the list in your wallet or diary and refer to it from time to time to check if your parachute is still in place.

## Avoiding ruts

After doing all the work we have suggested you do, it is important to keep on learning and not allow yourself to slip back into old habits. Often people work on themselves, develop self-awareness and other essential skills for life but then neglect to keep them up. So avoid getting into ruts and becoming complacent — even when things are going well.

Watch out for signs that the time has come to seek out a change of direction, and do not wait until change is forced upon you. Some of these 'pay attention' signals will come from within you, while others will be external. We list some of them below.

### Internal signals

- a readiness to face new challenges
- a sense of having been in the same job or done the same thing for too long
- a feeling of general malaise
- stress
- negative thoughts
- a sense of having learnt nothing new for a long time
- impatience and boredom with those around you at work .

## *External signals*

- an improved job market
- discord at home
- new boss
- cancelled meetings/appointments
- people apparently losing interest in you or your projects
- relocation
- a high degree of change in your organization
- major changes in your industry or sector
- technological change.

# Applied serendipity: looking for opportunities

The external signals warning you of change to come will not pose a threat so long as you are receptive to the opportunities that change may present. But do not wait for things 'out there' to determine your future path. Look for opportunities, even in unlikely situations. If for instance you find yourself in a dentist's waiting room, do not waste the time staring into space, but strike up a conversation with another patient or pick up a magazine you would not normally read.

It is a good idea to accept invitations even to events that appear uninteresting, because you never know who you might meet or what you might find out if you go. When you find yourself in a room full of people, whether it is at a social function, lecture or work-related meeting, use the opportunity to extend your network of contacts and find out whatever you can about other people. But do remember to show interest in *them*; see such meetings or encounters as an end in themselves, and the impression you leave will be favourable.

## *Activity 2: Learning not to miss opportunities*

Make a list of all the social functions, seminars, lectures, meetings and other events you have attended over the last six months. Consider which of these were missed opportunities to extend your network or learn something new.

Similarly, review the opportunities that are coming up over the next few months. Make plans, book places, enter dates in your diary. Over the next four months, aim to attend at least four events that you might otherwise have ignored.

## Case study: The man who manufactured his own luck

Harry is now 54 years old. Most of his working life had been spent in two blue-chip companies, and latterly he had been a senior manager in a large financial institution. A strategist and planner with an excellent grasp of information management, he had reached a position where he played a crucial role in decisions about the development of the organization's retail outlets and their supporting communication systems.

A take-over two years ago brought about a rationalization and restructuring of the organization. The new top management team offered all those over 50 very favourable redundancy terms and put gentle pressure on them to accept these terms. Prior to the merger, Harry had been planning how he wanted to spend the next phase of his life. His aim had been to 'retire' early to pursue a variety of interests: painting, travel and local politics. He also wanted to do some paid consultancy work and to spend more time with his wife, who had already decided to take early retirement from her post in a local school and teach part-time.

Throughout his career, Harry had been active in his professional society, holding the position of national president for two years. In addition, he represented the UK on an international professional body, which encouraged best practice throughout the world. His company had supported him in these activities, which enabled him to build up an extensive network of people in senior positions. Over the years tempting offers of consultancy work had come his way as a result of these contacts.

So when the opportunity to take redundancy arose, he took it — even though the company had been reluctant to let him go and offered him attractive terms to stay. Colleagues were surprised and some of those who would much rather have stayed could not understand his decision. But Harry knew what he wanted to do and felt that he now wanted to have more control over his time and his life.

Now, two years later, Harry is extremely happy and feels ten years younger. He has a satisfying balance of personal interests and paid assignments with considerable variety and scope. Some of his ex-colleagues look on his situation with envy. 'That's Harry,' said one. 'He always has been lucky.'

But Harry has actually manufactured his own 'luck'. He worked for a good degree in an area that interested him and he thought carefully about the organizations he wanted to work for. At a time when job change was relatively easy, he stayed in the second organization because he recognized that he would find it difficult to maintain the outside interests he had developed if he were to leave. And now that investment, apart from the value it added to his expertise at the time, is paying off handsomely in providing a valuable income stream which is preserving his pension almost intact.

Now look back at your own career history and think of occasions when you, like Harry, manufactured your own luck. Think also of opportunities you let slip by in the past and how you might make the most of similar occasions in the future.

## Be your own coach

If you have carried out the activities we have suggested in this book, you should be feeling the benefit of knowing yourself better and of having a clearer idea of where you are going. Your confidence in handling whatever comes up will be greater. But do not leave it there. Make it a habit to spend twenty minutes two or three times a week sitting quietly with a drink in a cafe — if you commute, do it on the way into work — jotting in your notebook, reflecting on the events of the week and your feelings about what is going on. It will be time well spent both in the continuing insights it will provide you and in the relaxation it will afford.

These insights will equip you for the next stage in your journey through life. If there is someone acting as your coach or mentor then you may wish to discuss your options and possible courses of action with that person, but remember that ultimately you have to be the judge of what is right and what is wrong for you. Do not wait for others to push you or tell you what do to. If you do not want to do something, the answer is not to do it. Trust your intuition and if something does not feel right, ask yourself why that is so, and then think of alternatives. As we said right at the beginning, IF IT IS TO BE, IT IS UP TO ME.

# FURTHER READING

We provide here a selection of books and articles that we have found useful in our work. We have grouped them under the following headings:

1. The Future of Work

2. Organizations and Development

3. Management Skills

4. Personal Change and Development

5. Job Change

## 1. The Future of Work

Barker, J (1992) *Future Edge*, Morrow, New York.

Bridges, W (1988) *Surviving Corporate Transition*, Doubleday, New York.

Bridges, W (1995) *Jobshift: How to Prosper in Workplace without Jobs*, Nicholas Brealey Publishing, London.

Drucker, P (1988) *Managing in Turbulent Times*, Harper & Row, New York.

Drucker, P (1993) *Post Capitalist Society*, Butterworth Heinemann, Oxford.

Handy, C (1991) *The Age of Unreason*, Century Business, London.

Handy, C (1994) *The Empty Raincoat: Making Sense of the Future*, Hutchinson, London.

Kanter, R (1992) *When Giants Learn to Dance*, Routledge, London.

Waterman, R, Waterman, J and Collard, B (1994) 'Toward a Career, Resilient Work- force', *Harvard Business Review*, July-August.

## 2.  Organizations and Development

Handy, C (1979) *Gods of Management*, Pan Books, London.
Handy, C (1993) *Understanding Organisations (4th edition)*, Penguin Books, Harmondsworth.
Harvey-Jones, J (1988) *Making It Happen: Reflections on Leadership*, Collins, London.
Herriot, P and Pemberton, C (1995) *Competitive Advantage Through Diversity*, Sage, London.
Kleiner, A, Roberts, C, Ross, R, Senge, P and Smith, B (1994) *The Fifth Discipline Fieldbook*, Nicholas Brealey, London.
Morgan, G (1986) *Images of Organisation*, Sage, Beverly Hills.
Pedler, M, Burgoyne, J and Boydell, T (1991) *The Learning Company*, McGraw-Hill, London.
Peters, T (1992) *Liberation Management*, Alfred Knopf, New York.
Senge, P (1990) *The Fifth Discipline*, Century, New York.

## 3.  Management Skills

Adams, J (1987) *Conceptual Blockbusting*, Penguin Books, Harmondsworth.
Cooper, C, Cox, C and Makin, P (1989) *Managing People at Work*, BPS Books, Leicester.
Harrison, J (1989) *Finance for the non-Financial Manager*, Thorsons, London.
Honey, P (1994) *101 Ways to Develop Your People Without Really Trying*, Peter Honey, Maidenhead.
Kennedy, G (1987) *Everything is Negotiable*, Arrow Books, London.
Lakein, A (1984) *How to Gain Control of your Time and your Life*, Gower Press, Aldershot.
Ohmae, K (1982) *The Mind of the Strategist*, McGraw-Hill, New York.
Pearson, B and Thomas, N (1991) *The Shorter MBA: A Practical Approach to Business Skills*, Thorsons, London.

## 4.  Personal Change and Development

Back, K, Back, K with Bates, T (1991) *Assertiveness at Work*, McGraw-Hill, London.
Boydell, T and Pedler, M (1985) *Managing Yourself*, Fontana, London.
Buzan, T (1982) *Use Your Head*, BBC Books, London.
Buzan, T and Buzan, B (1993) *The Mind Map Book*, BBC Books, London.
Cleese, J and Skynner, R (1983) *Families and how to Survive Them*,

Methuen, London.

Cleese, J and Skynner, R (1993) *Life and How to Survive it,* Methuen, London.

Cooper, C, Cooper, R and Eaker, L (1988) *Living with Stress,* Penguin, London.

Covey, S (1989) *The Seven Habits of Highly Effective People,* Simon & Schuster, New York.

Harris, T (1973) *I'm OK — You're OK,* Pan Books, London.

Honey, P and Mumford, A (1992) *The Manual of Learning Styles,* Peter Honey, Maidenhead.

Jeffers, S (1991) *Feel the Fear and do it Anyway,* Arrow Books, London.

Joyce, J (1992) *A Portrait of the Artist as a Young Man,* Mandarin Paperbacks, London.

Kolb, D, Rubin, I and McIntyre, J (1979) *Organisational Psychology: An Experiential Approach* (third edition) Prentice Hall, Englewood Cliffs, New Jersey.

McCormick, E (1990) *Change for the Better,* Unwin, London.

Robbins, A (1992) *Awaken the Giant Within,* Simon & Schuster, London.

Sheehy, G (1976) *Passages: Predictable Crises of Adult Life,* Bantam Books, New York.

Sheehy, G (1981) *Pathfinders,* Bantam Books, New York.

Stuart, C (1988) *Effective Speaking,* Pan Books, London.

Tanner, D (1990) *You Just Don't Understand,* Virago Press Ltd, London.

Turner, C (1994) *Born to Succeed: How to Release your Unlimited Potential,* Element Books, Shaftesbury, Dorset.

## 5. Job Change

Bolles, R (Pubished annually) *What Colour is Your Parachute?* Ten Speed Press, Berkeley.

Foster, T (1991) *101 Ways to Succeed as an Independent Consultant,* Kogan Page, London.

Golzen, G (1995) *Working for Yourself* (sixteenth edition), Kogan Page, London.

Johnson, R (1990) *The 24 Hour Business Plan: A step-by-step guide to producing a tailor-made business plan in 24 working hours,* Hutchinson Business Books, London.

Stevens, M (1989) *Winning at Your Interview,* Kogan Page, London.

Weldon, A (1994) *Breakthrough: Handling Career Opportunities and Changes,* Bene Factum Publishing, London.

# Index